Gaff Sail

The three-masted topsail schooner Esther Lohse *bound down the River Colne.*
She carries one square sail and represents one of the most successful forms of
fore and aft gaff sail plan evolved during the nineteenth century (Author).

**Naval
Institute
Press**

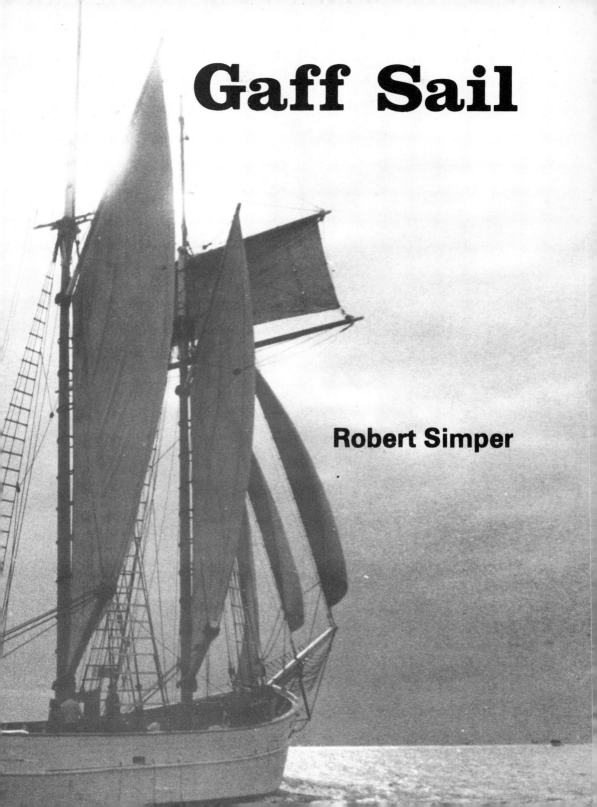

Gaff Sail

Robert Simper

Published and distributed in the United States of America by the
Naval Institute Press, Annapolis, Maryland 21402

First published 1980

ISBN 0 87021 827 1

Library of Congress Catalog Card No. 79-90907

To Bill Coke to whom these craft meant so much.

By the same Author:
Over Snape Bridge (1967)
Woodbridge & Beyond (1972)
East Coast Sail (1972)
Scottish Sail (1974)
North East Sail (1976)
British Sail (1977)
Victorian & Edwardian Yachting from Old Photographs (1978)

Cover photograph: *L'Atalanta* by Caroline Simper

Printed and bound in Great Britain

Contents

Introduction

The aim of this book is to provide a source of information on gaff craft. It is a wide range from the huge trading ships through small working craft to yachts and I am grateful to many experts of each type who have willingly given material to help further interest in gaff sail. Most people who have generously helped are mentioned in the text or photograph credits, but I would like to add to these: In America Norman Brouwer, Ted Miles and John M. Kochiss, in Australia Ron Parsons and in New Zealand Cliff Hawkins. In Denmark Michael Kiersgaard, in The Netherlands Ron van den Bos and Peter Dorleyn, in Germany Dr J. Meyer, Joachim Kaiser and Fr Cr Blaas.

In Britain many acknowledged authorities on local traditional craft and yacht design have given material. Particularly; from the English west country Michael Bouquet, East Anglian Broads John Perryman, Ireland Richard Scott, while Mrs Anne Pye made material available on *Moonraker's* cruises. Jim Lawrence for his views on sails. J. K. Ingham of the Seabird Association. In a way a book is like an iceberg with information and photographs showing up clearly above the surface, but the countless hours of background work is lost from view. I am particularly grateful to my wife Pearl for all the time she has willingly spent on this. Thanks also to Geoff Cordy for the all important photographic work.

R. S.
Ramsholt

53 ft (15.90 m) cutter Margeurite T *in 1974, taking part in an Old Gaffers Race on the* lmeer. *Built in 1893 she was originally one of the highly seaworthy pilot cutters which were* ated *in the Bristol Channel. Sold for a yacht in 1912 she was restored back to an elegant gaff* ty *by Les Windley of Cowes between 1970-74 (Heineken).*

CHAPTER ONE

Gaff Scene

In the age of working sail the gaff sail plan was the most universally popular for small craft throughout the western world. From the beginning of the nineteenth century until just after World War I most cargo traders and many fishing boats had gaff sails. Also almost all yachts through this long period were gaff. Yet the word gaff was never used to describe these craft. Craft were described as schooners, ketches, yawls, cutters and sloops and it was assumed that all had gaff sails. The four sided fore and aft sail was such a common feature of the shipping scene that it was completely taken for granted and then, quite quickly, completely forgotten.

To understand the gaff rig one must go back into the past, not all that far because this is not a rig of very great antiquity. To begin with the mariners of Northern Europe were for many centuries content with the square sail as the prime source of power. Indeed this developed into the highly complex and effective four masted barques of the late nineteenth century, but the square sail was an awkward thing to handle in a small boat. The Norse people knew that the square sail could sail closer to the wind if the forward leading edge could be kept tight. In time, and it took a long time, this became the lug and spritsail rigs. In spite of a great deal of research no one has definitely proved where and when the gaff sail first operated; however, the evidence suggests that it was developed by adding a spar to the head of the spritsail and then leaving the sprit ashore. This probably happened in the Netherlands during the seventeenth century. The next step was a boom to be added to the foot of the sail and here at last was an easy to control sail which would successfully beat to windward.

The gaff rigged craft made a tremendous contribution to the world transport during the critical period after the early discoveries when world trade was being developed. This contribution was not on the long and spectacular ocean routes but on the coastal and short sea voyages. The European settlers took the gaff rig to the furthermost corners of the globe. It was used to improve countless different types of craft in North America, Australia and New Zealand and where ever else the western world had strong connections. In fact for almost two centuries gaff sails propelled men about their work and pleasure without anyone considering it anything but normal. It was accepted that every craft was gaff unless otherwise stated.

By the middle of the eighteenth century the gaff cutter was regarded in Britain as being the most versatile rig for small craft. Its popularity is borne out in the meticulous sea scapes of the English maritime painter Charles Brooking (1723-59). The little gaff cutters Brooking used to add to his views of men-of-war are there to give atmosphere. Yet these cutters had the same basic sail plan as the numerous fishing smacks, pilot boats and yachts all over the British Isles right up to World War II. Of course the

The Norwegian Society for Saving of Lives at Sea commissioned the Larvik boatbuilder Colin Archer to build a series of sailing Rescue Ships. The first of these seen here was the 45 ft (13.90 m) Colin Archer built in 1893 which had 15 ft (4.65 m) beam 7 ft (2.30 m) draught and a sail area of 1184 sq ft (110 sq m). The 'redningskoite' became world famous for their ability to survive at sea and the Colin Archer (No 1) is now sailed and maintained by the Colin Archer Sailing Club (H. Sandvik).

The Gloucester, Mass, fishing schooner Frances P Mesquita, *built in 1905 has a large 'fisherman's' staysail set between the masts (Mystic Seaport Museum).*

eighteenth century gaff working boats were less sophisticated craft than the superb gaff craft built during the Edwardian period but the basic characteristics were unchanged.

The British developed the gaff cutter and by around 1800 were building vessels of 200 tons with this rig. They were used as naval dispatch boats, passenger packets and revenue cutters because they could beat against the wind better than a craft with a square rig. The cutters gave a good all round performance although they were not as fast off the wind as luggers, employed by smugglers and many fishermen. The British were rightly proud of the gaff cutter to the extent of calling it the 'national rig'. However the cutter did go out of favour to a certain extent after the 1850s when the schooner came to the fore. The reason for this was the improvement in the hull shape. The cutter of 1800 was a short beamy craft, even the 200 tonners were still only about 80 ft (24 m) long with a main boom of around 65 ft (19.5 m). In the struggle to produce faster craft, mainly for the rapidly growing sport of yacht racing, builders were discovering that long narrow hulls were more successful. This new breed of sleek hulled racer naturally had to have a longer main boom, but this huge spar proved to be unmanageable in strong winds. In yachts this lead to a change to the schooner rig and in fishing and cargo smacks they solved the problem by sawing the main booms off shorter and stepping a mizzen mast which created the ketch. By the 1870s it was regarded that the most successful size for a cutter was about 60 tons. After about 1890 the cost of maintaining a schooner caused many owners to revert to the cutter. The cutter yachts like the *Flame* and the 52 ft (15.6 m) *Forsa*, built in 1898 had totally different hull shapes to the cutters of a hundred years earlier.

North America was the stronghold of the schooner rig, mainly because on the Eastern Seaboard the prevailing winds meant that coastal passages were usually made on a broad reach which was the schooners best point of sailing. Yet for yacht racing the Americans also went over to huge cutters. Some of the proportions of these seem incredible now; the *Reliance* for instance had extending bow and stern which made her 202 ft (60.6 m) overall with a mainboom 114 ft (34.2 m) long. This overall length

The British racing cutter Flame *at the start of the Nore-Dover race in 1903. This Edwardian yacht has a jackyard topsail set (Author's Collection).*

The 52 ft (15.60 m) cutter Forsa *racing on the Clyde in 1898. A new yacht built by J. Reid & Co, Whileinch, to Alfred Mylne's design. Note the battens in the leech of the mainsail (Author's Collection).*

The Wilful, Champion *and* Pameta *in 1973 in the East Coast Old Gaffers Race. The 30 ft (9 m)* Champion *was built on traditional work boat lines by Kidby at Brightlingsea in 1936 while the 30 ft (9 m)* Wilful *was built by Sibbick of Cowes in 1899 as a yacht and originally had a round zinc lined cockpit. The* Wilful *has a large light weather 'ghoster' headsail set which is not as effective running as a spinnaker, but more useful on a broad reach. For beating to windward in a fresh breeze large jibs can simply bury the bows in the water (Author).*

The Morecambe Bay prawner Alice Allan. *This type was also known as a nobby and was used on the British coast between Cardigan Bay and the Solway Firth. Some smaller prawners built by Crossfield of Arneside in about 1912 were sold as yachts and about thirty of them raced as the Royal Mersey Yacht Club Rivers Class. The 35 ft (10.50 m) shrimping nobbies were fast, but they had low freeboard aft and when this was copied into the 24 ft (7.20 m) Rivers Class, racing men found that when pressed hard they could take water over the stern (Merseyside County Museums).*

The Galway hooker was a small but very capable craft used for carrying peat, general cargoes and passengers on the West Coast of Ireland. An annual race has now been started for the Connemara hookers now sailed as yachts at Mace near Carna and those taking part in 1977 were the 37 ft (11.10 m) Morning Star, *31 ft (9.30 m)* St John, *32 ft (9.60 m)* Hunter *and the* Volunteer *(Richard Scott).*

included the bowsprit. A similar racer, the *Vigilant* had a deck length of 124 ft (37.2 m). Most of the Yankee racers were about 70 ft (21 m) long but Thomas Fleming Day, Editor of the *Rudder* dubbed them 'leakabouts' which seems to sum up their seagoing qualities. These huge racing cutters were built on both sides of the Atlantic to a set of racing handicap rules which produced some very strange craft. The American Seawanhaka Measurement resulted in such racing freaks as the *Outlook* which was only 20 ft (6 m) on the waterline, 50 ft (15 m) overall, yet set 1800 sq ft (167 sq m) of sail. This would have been twice the sail area set by an ordinary working craft, even in the United States where large sail areas and speed were looked on as being a priority.

The curious results created by the early handicap system did not prevent some of the most talented designers from producing really outstanding craft. One of these was Nathaniel G. Herreshoff who was born at Bristol, Rhode Island in 1848. With his brother, 'Captain Nat' ran a boatyard at Bristol and at the same time he quietly designed more America's Cup winners than any other naval architect, largely because he had taken a degree in mechanical engineering. Nat Herreshoff was sometimes called a 'mathematical' designer, but in fact, designing a successful racer is largely an instinctive talent. Herreshoff first carved out a model hull of the future craft, this was the traditional approach to boat construction, but later he used mathematics to calculate the strength of the hull construction and produce a balanced sail plan.

Herreshoff had a wonderful eye for detail. He inspected his yard every morning and afternoon for over seventy years, only taking Sunday off in the summer when he went sailing. One of the marks of Herreshoff's designing was that he didn't just produce a drawing that would please a future owner, but also ones which other builders could follow easily. He trusted his own judgement above all. Once the Kaiser asked him to alter the dimensions of a planned yacht, but Herreshoff did not alter his plan for the German Emperor or anyone else.

Improvements to hull shape and sail plan went on through the Victorian period and finally this culminated in the golden era for the gaff rig between 1890-1914. This is a very hard fact to pin down, obviously outstanding craft were built before and after this period, but it is surprising how many yachts, former pilot cutters and other work boats from this period are still afloat and can hold their own against much newer craft. The gaff craft from before this era were practical but a little heavy to handle and rather plainer to look at. Those from the golden era have great style, particularly the Edwardian yachts. The quality of material and craftsmanship that went into these was

Here are some River Tagus barges leaving Lisbon Docks in 1971 bound inland with cargoes. These Portuguese craft are the last cargo carrying craft left working purely under sail in Europe. When stowing the gaff sail the lower part of the sail is brailed into the mast and the throat halliard kept fast, but the peak is let go so that the sail is folded down against the mast. The hold aft of the mast is open and presumably to avoid the danger of the mate falling in when light, the halliards lead down into the bow (Author).

the best that money could buy. The weak link in the gaff tribe at this time was the smaller yacht, these tended to be simply scaled down versions of the vast racing cutters.

The popularity of the gaff rig at this time was due to its versatility. It had been evolved in Northern and Western Europe because here the winds were constantly changing in direction and strength. The small craft sailors had to have a sail plan which could be quickly adapted to meet these restless wind changes. The gaff superiority in working boats was not seriously challenged until the early 1920s, when suddenly the lofty magnificent gaff sails were abandoned in favour of a motley collection of old car motors and primitive marine engines.

A useful barometer for measuring the state of gaff sail is the material published about it. The English Victorian writer, designer and committee man Dixon Kemp produced virtually the first standard reference book of the technical aspect with *A Manual of Yacht and Boat Sailing* (1878). Although a milestone in small boat literature he did not

Plan of the cutter yacht Osprey *built Brightlingsea in 1912.*

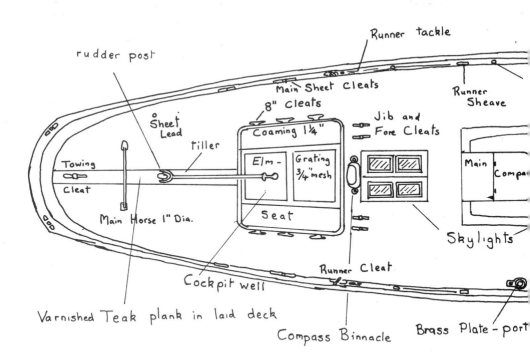

set out to in any way promote gaff sail, he simply recorded the contemporary yachting scene and suggested improvements. He was also heralding with his books an avalanche of yachting and boating literature which has been going on ever since. A friend of Dixon Kemps was R. T. McMullen (1830-91) whose first cruising book appeared in 1869. McMullen's *Down Channel* is a considerable insight into mid-Victorian gaff seamanship, for unlike most yacht owners of the period he actually comanded his own cruising yachts. Once when his two paid hands grumbled at Cherbourg, McMullen promptly paid them off and sailed his $19\frac{1}{2}$ ton *Orion* back to England single handed. This was a considerable achievement in seamanship because the *Orion* was no light weight twentieth century yacht bristling with gadgets, but a heavy sparred cutter with plenty of canvas which would have needed muscle power and skilled attention to control.

From Dixon Kemp onwards there has always been written information available on

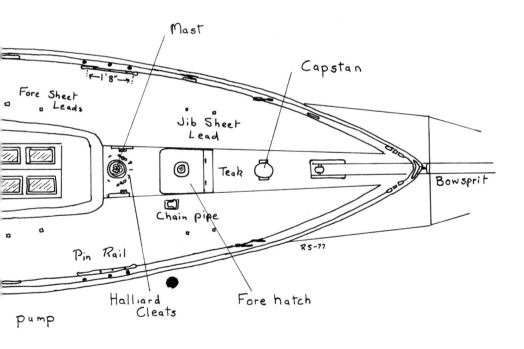

On the 70 ft (21 m) Breton tunny fisherman Biche, *built in 1935, two long rods can be seen; from each of these trailed eight fishing lines. Because they worked in the open Atlantic with its long seas the sail plan has been kept low to reduce rolling. She also draws 11 ft (3.30 m) aft and has 22 ft (6.60 m) beam. The* Biche *is still sailing as a charter craft from Poole and another South Coast charter ketch, the* Cleone *was built as the Ramsgate tosher (small trawling smack)* Fred & Dan *in 1920 (Seaward Marine).*

gaff seamanship. W. H. Rosser's *The Yachtsman's Handy Book* (1895) gives a wealth of detail that a master of a large Victorian gaff craft would have needed at sea. By the 1920s the bermudian rig had made a monumental impact on the racing scene while gaff yachts quietly faded away. Eric Hiscock remained faithful to the gaff with the engineless 4½ ton cutter *Wanderer II*, but in his book *Let's Go Cruising* (1946) he is beginning to think that the bermudian rig might also be adopted for cruising. Hiscock's *Cruising Under Sail* (1950) is largely devoted to technical details needed to maintain and sail a gaff cruiser, but by then the bermudian yachts get virtually the same coverage. John Leather's monumental *Gaff Rig* (1970) treats the subject in a completely different manner. In this the gaff sailed craft have become an object of historic interest with some suggestions of how the rig could be up-dated. It does contain

Some of the twenty seven Dutch owned Cornish Crabbers sailing on the Ijsselmeer at a Rally in 1977 with the three masted topsail schooner Charlotte Rhodes *in the background (Peter Keeling).*

The converted ship's lifeboat Nellie *is a gaff yacht with a jib on a Wykeham-Martin roller furling gear so that the sail can be stowed without any perilous foredeck work (Author).*

much more detailed references to working gear and rigging than many publications had before. Much of the information about gaff rigging had been forgotten at most boat yards, indeed the traditional knowledge needed to get a gaff boat ready for sea is now understood by enthusiastic owners, rather than designers and boat yards.

In this book the measurements given with the craft are the approximate lengths of the hull at deck level.

CHAPTER TWO

Regional Traders

In the North American coastwise fleet the use of gaff sail developed to propel some of the largest sailing ships ever built. In the nineteenth century the United States was still a new nation and had a continual stream of emigrants from Europe who were opening up the whole continent. There was expansion everywhere, particularly in the Eastern cities and this created an enormous demand for lumber for houses, shops and factories. This was a unique situation which really did not exist on such a large scale anywhere else in the world and this in turn created a demand for large sailing vessels with the minimum crew to haul bulk cargoes.

There were really two types of American freighting schooners, the local schooners and the multi-masters. The local schooners were mostly two-masters, often with centreboards which worked over short distances. A fairly typical example of this type is the 57 ft (17.10 m) schooner *Pioneer* now at the South Street Seaport Museum, New York. However she was built of wrought iron in 1885 which was very unusual for a North American freighter because timber was so plentiful, particularly in the New England states. Another type of local schooner was the three-masted Chesapeake Bay ram. Between 1889 and 1911 many baldheaded (no topmasts), centreboard rams were built to carry cargoes on the Chesapeake and Delaware Bays and more important to pass through the canal linking them. The 125 ft (37.50 m) 194 ton *Jennie D. Bell* carried cargoes until 1954 and finally sank at Salisbury, Maryland. The only one left is the 131 ft (39.30 m) *Edwin & Maud*, built in 1900 which is sailing as the Maine dude schooner *Victory Chimes*. She does not have an engine and is pushed or towed into port by her yawl boat. However Captain Fred Guild's incredibly smart *Victory Chimes* is America's largest commercial sailing vessel.

On the west coast of America the rapid growth of population produced another group of local schooners which brought lumber from the sawmills in the north western states to the cities for new homes. When this trade was taken over by the 'steam schooners' many West Coast lumber schooners were sold for fishing. These were either sailing to the Alaskan salmon fishery in the summer or to the Bering Sea as mother ships for one man dories, line fishing for cod. The last three cod fishermen were the *Charles R. Wilson, Wawona* and the *C. A. Thayer* which made their final voyages in 1946, 1947 and 1950 respectively. Two of these three-masters have been preserved; the 155 ft (46.50 m) *C. A. Thayer* is at San Francisco while the *Wawona* is at Kirkland, Washington.

The other American type of schooner was the multi-master. The demand for large bulk freights to be hauled over long distances precipitated the building of larger schooners. Over the years bigger wooden hulls with more masts left the country

The topsail schooner Flying Foam *of Bridgewater was built as* Marie *at St Malo, France in 1861.*
This schooner became the Flying Foam *in 1874 when bought by Noel of Jersey and was wrecked*
on Llandudno West Shore in 1936 where the hull disappeared into the sand within a few weeks.
In 1879 Noel had another schooner called Flying Foam *built by Le Huquet at Jersey and she was*
run down and sunk in 1900 (Beken).

shipbuilding yards in New England, but to keep the labour requirement down they had
gaff sails, seldom any square sails. However to get the heavy gaff sails aloft and to
work the anchor windlasses steam driven capstans were fitted. The multi-masted
schooners were not particularly attractive or fast but they were highly economical to
operate. Their main trades were hauling block ice and lumber from New England down
to the Eastern Seaboard cities and taking coal mostly from Newport News, Virginia to
the northern ports, particularly to feed the textile industry in New England. Multi-
masters also traded successfully to Europe and across the Pacific but not round Cape
Horn.

The British trading ketch Garlandstone *seen at New Ross, Southern Ireland in August 1940. Shortly before this Captain Andrew Murdock was at Courtmacsherry, Southern Ireland when his crew left him. Without any fuss 68 year old Captain Murdock made the voyage in war time across the Irish Sea single handed. He was four days and three nights with little rest from Courtmacsherry to Barry Roads. Here he borrowed a man from the schooner* Kathleen & May *to complete the passage to the Sevenside port of Lydney to load another freight of coal (Robert Shortall).*

The trading ketch Bessie Ellen, *Captain John Chichester, leaving Douglas, Isle of Man. This ketch was built at Plymouth in 1907 by W. S. Kelly. She was fitted with an engine in the mid 1920s and sold to Danish owners in 1947. At the time of her sale there were still twenty schooners and sixteen ketches left trading in the British Isles, mostly owned at Arklow in Wicklow and the Appledore area of North Devon (Michael Bouquet).*

The first schooner built with four masts was the 205 ft (61.50 m) *William L. White* in 1880. She was built at Bath, Maine which was then the centre of the American shipbuilding industry. Before the last four-master was built in 1921 over 450 had been built in the United States. In 1888 the first five-masters were built, one was the 831 ton *Louis* built on the Pacific coast at North Bend, Oregon and the other was the 1,778 ton *Governor Ames* built on the Atlantic coast at Waldoboro, Maine. The five-master was probably the most successful size for the multi-masted schooner and over fifty were built in Maine alone.

The schooners on the American coast were competing with the huge wooden lighters, with sails, which were towed by a tug. To meet this competition even larger multi-masted schooners were built. The great problem with the huge wooden hulls was to prevent the weight of the cargo from hogging them. This sagging effect was never completely overcome in wooden hulls. In the very end builders went over to steel hulls. The only American steel multi-masters were the five-masted *Kineo*, built by Sewells at Bath in 1903, the seven-masted *Thomas W. Lawson* built at Quincy, Massachusetts, in 1903 and the only seven-masted sailing ship ever built. She appears to have been a good money earner but was so large that she could only load coal at Newport News. Finally she was sent on a voyage to Europe in 1907 and was wrecked in the Scilly Isles. The year after the famous *Thomas W. Lawson* was built the six-masted *William L. Douglas* was launched at Quincy.

To collect coal the schooners from the Canadian Maritime Provinces used to go south to the United States with freights of lumber. Right into the 1930s these schooners from New Brunswick, Nova Scotia and Newfoundland were referred to as 'British'. Canada was still considered to be the inland province of Ontario and Quebec. The Maritime Provinces schooners differed very little from the United States equivalent except that they were usually smaller since their trade was mostly to small settlements. The Canadians called a three-master which had masts all the same height a tern schooner; the term came from poker playing, meaning three of a kind.

The North American schooners, whether fishing or freighters, carried a far larger sail area than their European equivalents. There was plenty of fog and sometimes ice around the Grand Banks, but generally speaking the wind conditions were not as fierce as on the North American side of the Atlantic. The Gloucester type was owned in ports from New York to Newfoundland which shows they were very suitable for the area, but on the few occasions when fishing schooners came over to the British Isles they found themselves over-sparred and over-canvassed. However it made commercial sense to own a fast schooner because they were often sailed long distances between fishing grounds and markets. The legendary *Bluenose*, although built to race, was so fast that she could make three trips to the Banks in the same time that it took other schooners to do two. In 1977 there were only thirty real Gloucestermen left either as draggers (trawlers), yachts, houseboats or other uncertain roles. Many were built to compete against power vessels. The *Nina W. Corkum* was built in 1922 at Lunenburg, Nova Scotia to race, but was beaten by the *Bluenose* in the Canadian trials. The 155 ft (46.50 m) knockabout (no bowsprit) schooner *Robert J. Knickle* built at Lunenburg in 1926 was, like many more of her type, sold to the Caribbean for freighting in her old age. The *Theresa E. Connor* built at Lunenburg in 1938 was the last Canadian schooner to go dory fishing. Her last trip to the Banks was in 1963 but her crew were all then too old and no young men wanted to spend their days tossing about in tiny dories line fishing for cod. The last American schooner to carry a mainsail was the *Lady of Good Voyage*, built at Ipswich, Massachusetts in 1941, while the *Puritan* built in 1944 at Thomaston, Maine was the last American working schooner to carry sail.

Most American owners gave up sailing schooners in the 1930s and switched to draggers, but the Canadians developed a large diesel-sail schooner which had the classic appearance of a Gloucesterman, but was much more beamy. These were knockabout schooners which carried only a low sail plan of two headsails, a gaff foresail and triangular trysail on the main mast. The Canadian motor sailers were very

The Gloucester mackeral fishing schooner Arthur James *sails on her maiden trip in 1905. She had been built by J. F. James at Essex, Mass. and represents a typical Gloucesterman of the 1895-1905 period. On deck can be seen the seine boat which was used for laying out the purse-seine net. At sea there would have been a man aloft looking for mackeral shoals (Mystic Seaport Museum).*

versatile, they went to the Grand Banks fishing or served as coastal or Caribbean cargo traders. The coasts of Nova Scotia and Newfoundland were dotted with tiny isolated fishing hamlets and the motor schooners took mixed cargoes along the coast. After unloading fuel in barrels, building materials and any other type of goods, they loaded dry salt fish which was the main cash earner for these tiny communities. The last Canadian knockabout motor schooner built to carry a full sail plan was the 93 ft (27.90 m) *Norma & Gladys* built by four Newfoundland fishermen at Trinity Bay in 1945. Like the 131 ft (39.30 m) *Francis Geraldine* built at Lunenburg in 1944 the *Norma & Gladys* went fishing for a few years and then switched to freighting until road transport became too competitive. In 1973 the *Norma & Gladys* was bought by the Province of Newfoundland to promote a 200 mile fishing limit and better management of fish stocks.

The North American schooner was greatly admired in Europe where a similar sail plan was used by yachts rather than work boats. However pilots found the two-masted schooner a practical rig. The Dutch had pilot schooners serving Rotterdam, Ijmuiden and Den Helder and the German North Sea ports also had schooners. In 1912 the last

The Gloucester 'clipper' schooners of 1870-90s carried a huge sail plan with long jib booms. Because so many men were lost, the pole bowsprit like the one on the Arthur James *were introduced. The next step was to do away with the 'widow making' bowsprit by extending the bows. The first knockabout or Indian head schooner was the* Helen B. Thomas *built by Oxner & Story, Essex, Mass. This is another of their knockabout schooners, the* Thomas A. Cromwell *built in 1905. She has dories on deck and the huge Grand Bankers anchor with its wooden stock on the bow (Mystic Seaport Museum).*

of these built was the superb 96 ft (28.80 m) steel *Emden*. She had to survive the bad temper of the North Sea and therefore there were no portholes in the sides which could let water in by being left open or smashed. The bulwarks were high and even then her few skylights and companionways were central so that in a knock down squall water could not get into the hull. A number of schooners had been swamped so that the final development of the North Sea pilot schooner was the result of long hard practical experience. A good all round handiness was more desirable than outright speed, the *Emden* could average eleven knots. She was eventually lost as Windjammer Cruises *Yankee* in 1964 when the anchor chain snapped.

In Britain the most famous pilot boats were the gaff cutters used in the Bristol Channel, but the Liverpool pilots used schooners which were very close in design to the Victorian yachts. A little further north the pilots at Fleetwood had schooners, notably the clipper bowed *Falcon*, built 1894. The Barrow pilots bought the hull of a fishing smack built at Fleetwood in 1880 and fitted her out as the schooner *Albicore*. She was a familiar sight on station near the Morecambe Bay lightship until being broken up in 1923.

The two and three-masted schooners were used extensively in coastal and North Atlantic trades by the British, but virtually always square topsails were carried on the foremast. These were known as topsail schooners, while the Victorian schooner yachts with fore and aft topsails above the gaff sails were sometimes called double topsail schooners. The large gaff mainsail, which on a two-masted schooner is the aft most sail, and the square topsails were a very powerful combination for sailing just off the wind. However the huge mainboom was a problem to control in heavy seas. The next stage was for the boom to be cut short and a small mizzen mast stepped. The three-masted topsail schooner was easier to handle because the sails were smaller. This meant that reefing was much simpler because to reduce sail area another sail could be stowed. Of course with square sails set the schooner could not point so close to the wind, but this was not considered a disadvantage since speed through the water was the most important. It was found that a schooner with square sails set got to its destination quicker than an ordinary schooner which only sagged to lo'ward (leeward) if not kept moving fast. However if the square topsails were stowed the yards aloft still created so much windage that they were trimmed as if the sails were set.

When the returns from small sailing cargo ships started to fall the pattern was for the square sails to be replaced by a small auxiliary engine. Then to further reduce the number of hands needed many schooners were altered to ketches. In the end better road

The Norma & Gladys *of St Johns, Newfoundland has the pole mast and two headsails knockabout rig of the later Canadian schooners (Author).*

The American three masted schooner City of Augusta *was built at Bath, Maine in 1880 and when sold to Cuba in 1918 was renamed* Lucia *(Author's Collection).*

The four-masted schooner Marie Gilbert *of New London, Conn. just after launching at Mystic in 1906. Barely a year later she was lost at Masson Bar, Mayport, Florida (Author's Collection).*

transport robbed the small traders of their modest livelihood, but some trades such as coal across the Irish Sea and the Bristol Channel remained a stronghold for motor sailers. The topsail schooner *Nellie Bywater* was kept going for many years by the cabin table management of her owner Captain McKibbin of Annalong, a tiny port in County Down on the Irish Sea coast of Ulster. Captain McKibbin would buy potatoes from the local farmers, take them across to Liverpool and sell them. Next he bought coal at Garston and sailed back to Kilkeel or Annalong and sold it. Finally the cash that was created by this transaction was shared out between the vessel and the crew. In the shipping slump of the early 1920s most schooners and ketches were made almost too expensive to operate, though through shear hard work and enterprise owners at some of the small ports with a strong tradition for schooner management were able to buy up vessels at knock down prices and put them back into trade. At the Irish port of Arklow, just south of Dublin several families ran motor schooners for decades after they had vanished from similar places.

Most Arklow schooners were clipper bowed, counter sterned vessels built back in the 1880-90s, but Irish owners also bought up the iron 126 ft (37.80 m) three masted schooner *Gaelic* and *Cymeric* which had been built at Amlwch to carry Welsh slate in deepwater trades. Hall of Arklow bought the 116 ft (34.80 m) steel three master *De Wadden,* built at Waterhuizen, The Netherlands in 1917, also the Dutch built 112 ft (33.60 m) steel *Venturer* came under the Irish flag. The enterprising Arklow owners designed motor schooners which were easy to handle in docks yet could make use of a

The American East Coast five masted schooner Cora F. Cressy, *built at Bath, Maine in 1902 still exists as a hulk in Maine. The only schooner of this type left afloat is the* Elizabeth Bandi *built at Gulfport, Mississippi in 1919 for the coasting trade and she is now the barque* Seute Deern *at Bremerhaven, Germany (National Maritime Museum).*

fair wind at sea. At Arklow two wooden schooners, the 86 ft (25.80 m) *J.T.&S.* (the name came from her owners John Tyrrell & Son) and the 92 ft (27.60 m) *Invermore* were built in 1921 on the lines of fishing boats. These had no bowsprits, straight stems, three pole masts and cruisers sterns. Fitted with petrol engines they traded with coal from the River Mersey across to Dublin and along the Irish coast. They were more functional than beautiful.

Coal and cattle food from South Wales ports to North Devon kept alive another group of motor schooners and ketches owned in Appledore and Braunton, both on the estuaries inside the Bideford Bar. In fact the few British trading schooners still afloat survived because they became part of the Bar fleet. The *Eilian* was still trading as a motor coaster in Denmark in 1977 and the three masted topsail schooner *Result* was awaiting restoration at Belfast. The only one whose future is at least a little secure is the lovely wooden three masted topsail schooner *Kathleen & May* which is now preserved by the Maritime Trust but even they are having a hard job maintaining such a large wooden vessel. The ketch *Garlandstone* is at a privately owned museum in Porthmadog, Gwynedd, while the ketches *Irene* and *Emily Barratt* are houseboats on the River Thames although *Irene* does make summer cruises. The little ketch *Isabel* set off on a world cruise in 1974. A more secure future should be in store for the ketch *Bessie Ellen*, built at Plymouth in 1907 after being rebuilt at Troense, Denmark. The trading smack *Marie* built at Salcombe in 1904 was still afloat in 1968, she had become a gravel barge at Appledore. Actually there were Taw and Torridge gravel gaff sloop barges which worked in these rivers. The last one built to sail was the *JJRP* by Philip Waters at Appledore in 1923 and she is now being restored.

The two and three masted schooners were widely used in Northern Europe but each country had its own distinct variety. In The Netherlands they never built wooden

The American West Coast five masted schooner Blanca, *built in 1919 was one of many such schooners built to replace World War I losses.* Blanca's *captain is trying out a highly original raffee topsail (National Maritime Museum).*

OPPOSITE

The American West Coast schooner Inca, *built 1896. Like most of the schooners from the Pacific coast she has a triangular sail set aft (National Maritime Museum).*

schooners, but in the province of Groningen many steel 'schoener' were built on the waterway which links the city of Groningen with the sea at Delfzijl. The tweemast (two-masts) schoener had masts of the same height while similar eenmast (one-mast) schoener carried a very lofty sail plan. The three-masted *San Antonio* built in 1909 was the first Dutch schooner built with an engine, but still launched with figurehead and open steering wheel. She is now the Hamburg cruise schooner *Ariadne*.

Many steel schooners were also built in Germany, particularly by Lühring at Brake on the River Weser. The Lühring family yard started in the 1850s and by the late 1890s were turning out two more or less standard types; small two-masted schooners with a light yard on the foremast for a running square foresail set flying — the 'money-bag' of the British schoonermen. The larger type of three masted schooner crossed four yards on the foremast. Many of this type traded down to the River Plate in South America. One of these, the 117 ft (35.10 m) *Marie Linnemann*, built 1908 was seized as a prize after World War I and became the British *S.F. Pearce* of Fowey. Even after the Great War German owners still had confidence in sail and began ordering new schooners from Lühring's yard such as *Achim Griese* in 1921 although the last schooner built shortly afterwards was the *Conrad Lühring*. Although in 1932 the three masted motor schooner *Aar* of Hamburg was launched.

In 1911 Lühring launched five of their steel two masters and one of these was bought by a British-Australian group in 1974 who refitted her at Faversham, England as the brigantine *Eye of the Wind*. This 90 ft (27 m) schooner is reputed to have made two voyages to the River Plate before World War I. In 1922 she was sold as the *Merry* to Swedish owners and was fitted with her first engine four years later. Her next role was fishing for herring off Iceland from Gronsund on the Swedish West Coast. In the early 1950s she went aground and the owner was lost overboard. The result of this disaster was that her bottom plates were renewed before she resumed trading.

The German three-masted schooner Margarethe *with a deck cargo of timber (R. W. Cowl).*

    In North West Europe the most successful forms of fore-and-aft cargo vessels for
long hauls were the topgallant schooners. Basically they were fore-and-aft schooners,
usually three-masted, with three square sails on the foremast. This combined the low
labour requirement of the three-masted schooners with the powerful driving power of
the square sails. The topgallant schooners began gaining popularity in around 1870 and
were most numerous in the ocean trades in the 1890s. In Britain this rig was most
favoured in the small ports of Western England and Western Wales which sent ships
across the North Atlantic to Newfoundland and to the Mediterranean. At the Welsh
slate port of Porthmadog the three shipbuilding yards at the top of the harbour
produced a series of these clipper schooners between 1889 and 1913. These made smart
passages and earned their share holders good money so long as their wooden hulls
could stand the hard driving.

CHAPTER THREE

Ketches and Schooners

In Denmark the wooden schooners fitted into the economy of small shipping communities. They could be built of local materials on any piece of ground at the edge of water deep enough to slide in a new hull without damaging it. The cost of building and fitting out a hull could be covered by the merchants and sea captains in the immediate area. Often in small yards there were years between laying the keel and the craft being ready for sea, but once completed they were capable of sailing virtually anywhere in the world. This versatility was the strong point of the gaff sail and was part of the secret why Western sailing craft were the first to voyage all over the globe.

All the Danish ports had small sailing ships, but in the tideless Østersöen (Baltic) ports scattered on islands to the south of Fyn a tremendous ship owning economy based on schooners was created. An ancient right had given the island of Aerö the sole right to trade with German towns and this laid the basis for the schooner fleet to build up. Marstal, which did not even have a proper harbour until a stone breakwater was built, became the centre of the Aerö schooner fleet. At Marstal virtually every krona possible was saved to go back into more ships. It was said that no seagulls ever bothered to follow a Marstal ship because nothing was ever thrown overboard. Also sailors had difficulty in working the sails because it was alleged that the ropes were always cut too short. Never mind what other people thought, it seems that from the smallest jagt to the finest deepwater barquentine, at its peak something like three hundred sailing vessels of all sizes hailed from the little town of Marstal.

The typical inter-island trader of the early 1800s was the jagt. A single masted craft with a flat sloping transom stern and round bows. In Denmark the same hull with a topmast and gaff topsail became a sluup. Just as in Britain many trading smacks were cut in half and lengthened and went to sea again as ketches, in Denmark also the jagts were lengthened and became ketches which were called galeases. This type had so much buoyancy that new schooners were built on the same lines and were known as jagtbygget (jagt-built). They were also known as Marstal-built although there is no evidence that this type really originated there. Eventually the jagt-built hull was used throughout Denmark, Sweden and the Baltic coast of Germany which then included modern Poland. The *Lail* which is a jagt-built German schooner is still sailing, but she was built to carry fresh fruit from Morocco. The jagt-built Danish schooners and galeases were also trading regularly to Newfoundland and Greenland so that it was not just a coastal hull form.

The other Scandinavian hull type had a clipper bow and counter stern and was known as klipperbygget (clipperbuilt). Usually the large schooners were clipperbuilt, but there was no set pattern. A builder would produce which ever type of hull the future

The Danish three-masted bramsejlskonnert (topgallant schooner) Ellen *of Marstal. This 305 ton steel vessel was built at Marstens Hook, The Netherlands (Danish Maritime Museum, Kronborg Castle).*

owners ordered. The credit for introducing the clipper hull into Southern Fyn is given to J. Ring Andersen who served an apprenticeship building clippers at Alex Hall's famous yard in Aberdeen and then returned to build his first ship at Svendborg in 1862. In the age of sail there were 22 different building vaerft (wharves) in Svendborg and the neighbouring villages of Troense and Thurø which are just across The Sound. Shipyards flourished there because there was a plentiful supply of Danish oak and deep water for launching, while many of the other tideless Danish Baltic ports are very shallow.

At the peak of the schooner era around 400 small ships were owned in the Svendborg area. The general rule was that Svendborg ships traded with timber from Sweden or Finland to Britain or Northern France. The time on passage from Finland to a North Sea port was between six to eight weeks and the schooners then returned to the Baltic ports with coal from Britain. In the schooner's day most of the Baltic ports iced up in the late winter so that many returned home to be laid up there. Due to the movement of the Gulf Stream the northern waters have become less severe, but most of the wooden motor schooners which were built later were coated with metal sheets on their sides to protect them against ice. Some Svendborg schooners spent the winter taking a freight to the Mediterranean, usually clay from Cornwall to Italy.

The Marstal ships also carried timber from the vast Swedish and Finnish forests to British ports, but they were much more inclined to go deep sea. Schooners left the

The Danish three-masted topgallant schooner Lindhardt. *Clipper built at Thuro in 1902 she is seen here with the neutral marks on during World War I, but she was still sunk by a German torpedo in the Atlantic in 1917 (Danish Maritime Museum, Kronborg Castle).*

shelter of Marstal's breakwater and found their way through the narrow channels between the islands and eventually out into the open sea and then across the Atlantic to load salt cod in tiny Newfoundland settlements for the Latin Countries. They went south to the Carribean or to some lonely Central American river to collect mahogany. Some went north to Iceland and loaded salt cod for as far away as Egypt but odd Marstal traders ventured round Cape Horn although generally they kept away from that sailor's hell.

The schooner fleets of the Svendborg and Marstal area reached such proportions that every spring when the timber traders were fitting out anything up to 2,000 young men from all over Northern Europe would flock into the towns in search of a berth on them. In World War I Denmark remained neutral, but because so many of her ships were trading to British ports the German Navy sank many of them. Marstal alone lost over thirty large barquentines and schooners and between 1919-22 about twelve new ones were built as replacements. War losses created a boom in freight rates and Danish owners started to order four-masted schooners. All were clipper built vessels and some of these were topsail schooners. Unlike the three-masted schooners which were such a success, the larger four-masters built of heavy Danish oak were inclined to roll excessively on the North Atlantic passages. Most of these had short careers, usually ending up by going missing at sea.

This four-masted Danish skonnert (schooner) Drogden *was built at Svendborg in 1917 (Danish Maritime Museum, Kronborg Castle).*

The world depression of the early 1920s hit the Danish small deepwater sailers very hard. There was simply not enough work for them and many were sold to Sweden and Finland as coasters. The remaining Marstal schooners were often forced to spend long periods laid up but when ever possible they were back wandering the seas where ever they could fix a freight. During three years in the early 1930s the three-masted topgallant schooner *Merkur* visited Syria, Portugal, Sweden, Norway, Ireland, Scotland, Newfoundland and the West Indies. Another three-masted schooner the *Hertha* spent a whole year on the Newfoundland coast and then in 1934 crossed to Oporto, Portugal with salt cod in 22 days. The last Marstal four-masted schooner was the *Alfa* which was sold in 1935. In the 1970s the long Marstal waterfront is no longer a forest of masts as it was in the early 1900s. Only yachts are there now, but small Marstal owned and crewed power vessels are still working all over the world.

Before World War I Danish wooden sailing vessels were being fitted with 'helpmotors' and by the early 1930s there were about sixteen Marstal motor schooners. The introduction of engines far from killed sail, actually it prolonged the Danish inter-island and Greenland traders which were true auxiliaries because they used both sail and power on passage. Several yards continued to build wooden vessels which were launched with both sail and power. Ring Andersens at Svendborg produced the jagt built galease 85 ft (25.50 m) *Grethe* (now the brigantine *Romance*) in 1936 and her sister ship the *Dagny* the following year. However the final motor sailers built in

The fornagter (fore-and-aft) schooner I.P. Thorsøe *was built at Frederikshavn in 1902. This Northern Danish fishing port was the home of a fine fleet of shapely double ended fishing ketches and this may be why the* I.P. Thorsøe *has a deep fine lined hull (Danish Maritime Museum, Kronborg Castle).*

Denmark were really a new type. This was due to the design of Karl Lorentzen who ran away to sea before World War I and after going to America in a German full rigged ship spent some time working on the Gloucester type of Grand Banking schooners which he much admired. In the late 1930s when he ordered a new vessel from Ring Andersen he produced a design which incorporated some features of a Grand Banker but of course for a Baltic trader it had to be much more shallow draught. The result was the galease 98 ft (29.40 m) *Havet* (now West German *Seute Deern II*) built in 1938. She is regarded as being the best of Ring Andersen's later craft and appears to have had finer lines and much more cut away forefoot than the others. After *Havet* came a steady line of similar traders with round counter sterns and sharp bows. In 1942 came the two-masted schooner *Talata* which in 1977 left Svendborg again, rerigged as the three-masted topsail schooner *Mercandic II*. The *Lehnskov* of 1943 was sunk by a mine. The *Nette S* of 1944 became the *Prince Louis II* and now *Bel Espoir II*. The *Lars* of 1945 was back at Ring Andersen's yard on the tiny island in Svendborg harbour in 1977 to be fitted out as the French three masted topsail schooner *Caréne*. On the quay beside her lay a complete set of new wooden spars. Svendborg had by this time become the centre of the remaining traditional sailing craft in Scandinavia and that spring no less than nine sailers had laid there.

The galease *Ring Andersen* built in 1948 is regarded as being the last trading motor sailer built in Denmark. In 1950 came the tubby topsail schooner *Lilla Dan* built as a training ship. However the *Mona* of 1951 was another of the *Havet* (ocean) type. She

The Mercandic II *has been fitted out as a traditional three-masted topsail schooner and even carries a main topmast staysail (East Anglian Daily Times).*

later traded as the motorship *Activ* and finally was taken to Michael Kiersgaard's Jacobsens Plads yard at Troense for conversion back to sail. The first known record of the launching of a cargo ship at this yard was in 1708 and building went on right up to the last schooner in 1920. One vessel built there was the *Noah* in 1903 which later became better known as the three-masted topsail schooner *Artemis*. By the road above Jacobsens Plads overlooking the peaceful Sound between the islands of Taasing and Thurø are the attractive houses built by sailing ship masters. Danish sea captains spent a lifetime wandering the seas and then returned to the islands to pass away their time fishing from small boats.

In the mid 1960s more road bridges in Denmark allowed road transport to start taking freights away from the inter-island motor schooners and galeases. All round the Baltic literally hundreds of small wooden and a few steel traders bought from Germany and The Netherlands, suddenly came on the market and a steady stream of them left, destined for various roles all over the western world. An English couple, Lt-Cdr Peter Baker and his wife Patsy, bought a Danish fishing boat and went back later and bought the three-masted schooner *Als*. Since she proved to be too large for two people to maintain and handle they sold the *Als* and in 1972 bought the 68 ft (20.40 m) *I.P. Thorsøe* which is one of the very few Baltic traders to have kept the same name throughout her career. After being rerigged as a charter ketch based at Dartmouth *I.P. Thorsøe* proved to be fast and she once averaged eight knots on passage under sail from

Peter Baker at the wheel of the I.P. Thorsøe. *The unusual solid brass wheel was fitted when launched and had previously been on a vessel which had been wrecked. The stern davits are typical of the Baltic traders and were even used by the jagt-built schooners which traded to South America (Author).*

Milford Haven round Land's End to Falmouth. In between filming the 'Onedin Line' television series the *I.P. Thorsøe* left the three-masted topsail schooner *Charlotte Rhodes* some eight miles astern in an informal race from Gloucester (Sharpness) to Milford Haven. The *Charlotte Rhodes* is an ex Newfoundland trader and in a long sea passage her size would probably have given her an advantage.

A former Danish trader which has made some smart passages is the 94 ft (28.20 m) three masted topsail schooner *Esther Lohse*. She was built at Hobro in 1941 and later spent eleven years in the Greenland and Icelandic trades. She was bought by British owners in 1973 and four years later, skippered by Anthony Davies left the Bristol Channel after doing some film work at Gloucester and averaged $9\frac{1}{2}$ knots under sail in near gale force winds on the over 500 mile passage back to the Thames Estuary.

In Copenhagen the old sailors quarters at Nyhavn has been reserved as berths for the restored traditional craft. In London St Katherine's Dock, near Tower Bridge encourages historic craft to berth there while at Hamburg the Oevelgoenne Museumshafen is another base for restored working craft. Some of these are the ewer barges which were developed from double ended norse craft to work on the River Elbe which flows through marshlands from Hamburg some fifty miles down to the North Sea. The ewers had flat bottoms to sit on the mud at low water, but above this their

The Danish built Esther Lohse *was found to be well balanced under this sail plan after she was given a raffee topsail forward to balance the mizzen (Author).*

hulls had flared sides so that they would sail. The fracht (cargo) ewers had wide deep transom sterns and were tiller steered. Most of them traded in the Elbe carrying potatoes and grain to Hamburg. The large ketch rigged See Ewers traded to Denmark and Sweden and early ones even undertook voyages to The Netherlands and England. Many of the Besan Ewers had a 'roof' (deckhouse galley) just forward of the besan (mizzen) mast. The Fischer Ewers often had such shapely lines above the flat bottom that they did not need leeboards. Finkenwerder and Altenwaerder, two low islands just below Hamburg were famous for their Fischer Ewers which fished in the Elbe and the Watt off the German North Sea coast.

The ketch rig is not as efficient as the cutter or schooner but by having smaller sails the ketch was easier to handle. The French Icelandic fishermen abandoned their 'goëlettes' (topsail schooners) in favour of 'dundees' (ketches) because although smaller, they were easier to control and not having so much gear aloft had a better motion in a heavy seaway. Some of the most attractive working ketches produced in the western world were to be found on the Australian coast. In Colonial Australia the very sparsely scattered population was mainly in small settlements near the coast. The settlers naturally looked to the sea as a link between the colonies and the outside world. Much of Australia was very dry and lacked shipbuilding timber except for the island of Tasmania which was first colonised in 1804. English settlers built the first craft on the

The 60 ft (18 m) galease Marie *of Altona was built at the Danish Baltic port of Faaborg in 1898 and was restored for German owners in 1973-74. The square cut yard topsail presents a large area of sail for off the wind sailing, but is not so effective for close hauled sailing. Many trading ketches replaced this old fashioned yard topsail after about 1910 by a jib-headed topsail which went on a wire to the main mast head and so held the luff taut which allowed it to keep drawing when sailing close hauled (Author).*

lines of Thames barges with gaff sails and leeboards. The craft built between 1817-49 were basically the same types as were being built in England during the same period, but in the 1850s leeboards were abandoned and centreboards became the general practice. Later a pronounced clipper bow was introduced. Probably the bow, like the centreboards, were brought by Americans from the Eastern United States or they could have resulted from the influence of the small wooden clipper ships being built at Hobart for the London trade. The Hobart ketches always retained the flat bottom and sides of the Thames barge because they loaded off beaches and they were also usually referred to as barges by the men who sailed them. In the 1850s trade with the colonies of Victoria and South Australia began to increase and this meant crossing the stormy Bass Strait. The barge hulls had to be improved enough to give good windward qualities to make the Bass Strait crossing. Thus the late nineteenth century 'Tassie' ketches were about 68 ft (20.40 m) long and had one ton centreboards which when lowered projected some eight feet below the hull. They were great sail carriers. The *Annie Watt* built at Port Esperance, Tasmania in 1870 was 63 ft (18.90 m) long, 18 ft (5.40 m) beam and 5 ft 6 in (1.65 m) draft without a centreboard yet carried 4000 sq ft (371.61 m) of sail and is credited with making 10 knots in a good breeze.

The Tasmanian ketches often had the appearance of yachts with their white hulls and actually raced in the Royal Hobart Regatta. The first barge race was sailed in 1848 and the last race was sailed in 1951 when the *May Queen*, built on the Huon River in 1867 won. Many ketches were built with fine lines with an eye to being the winner which allowed them to have the coveted gilded rooster at the masthead for the following year.

This is a Besan-See (mizzen-seagoing) Ewer seen in about 1914. These German tiller steered barges traded along the North Sea coast. The Danish Evert barges were virtually the same and traded to North Sea coastal islands (Fr Cr Blaas).

The Hobart ketches carried huge jackyard topsails (club topsails in America) and there were several cases where heavy squalls rushing down hot valleys capsized the well canvassed ketches. Even the three-masted schooner *Alciro* had three jackyard topsails at one stage, but in the 1930s the Tasmanian and South Australian ketches had been fitted with the easier to handle jib headed gaff topsails.

The South Australian ketches and schooners traded from Port Adelaide to the lonely farming outposts on two gulfs, Kangaroo Island and the West Coast. In the 1930s a regular feature was taking grain out to the square riggers in Spencer Gulf which then went to Europe.

Many of the smaller Tasmanian ketches were fitted with wells and went crayfishing. A 20 ft boat was carried on the deck and was used for laying the pots. Some really beautiful 70 ft (21 m) clipper bowed ketches, similar to the trading ketches but with a keel and finer lines, were built for the Bass Strait fishery. Square sails were used very little on the Australian coast because of the difficulty of getting the extra labour to handle them. However there were some fine gaff vessels which carried square canvas such as the *Alma Doepel* built as a three masted topsail schooner on the Bellinger River, New South Wales, in 1903. Compared to the square riggers the gaff craft called for much less sail handling when beating to windward, but when running off the wind over long distances the square riggers had the advantage. This was why so many gaff trading craft incorporated some square sails. The topsail schooner could be turned into a brigantine for down wind sailing by fixing a temporary square foresail. The fashion used by the New Zealand schooners such as the famous *Hally Bayley* and the *Huia* was

Hobart ketches just before the start of the annual race in 1937. In Europe the ketch evolved from adding a small mast on to a cutter so that the mizzen was never a very important sail. In North America the fishing methods meant that the schooners had huge crews and that much of their speed was derived from simply carrying a lot of sail. The Australians wanted a craft with the speed of a schooner, but with low labour requirements of a ketch. The result was a ketch with a very large mizzen and this was really the most practical form of two masted gaff sail (State Library of South Australia).

The 'barge' Adonis *of Hobart built 1864, has had her topmast removed (State Library of South Australia).*

to have a kind of half square sail on a wire under the mainyard which could be hauled to windward from the deck rather like a curtain being moved across. Many single masted craft carried a square sail, but in the 1920s this was replaced in yachts by a triangular running sail boomed out by a pole at the foot.

There was considerable trade for small sailing ships loading timber in Kaipara Harbour in New Zealand's North Island and taking it some 1000 miles (1609 kilometres) across the Tasman Sea to Australia. The New Zealand scows also loaded sawn timber at Kaipara mills and went through the fierce waters of Cook Strait into the bar harbours on the South Islands west coast. Since Victorian New Zealand had very few quays or wharves most cargoes had to be loaded on the open beaches. This caused the development of the New Zealand scow which was probably the most advanced form of sailing barge produced anywhere in the world.

The first scow in New Zealand was launched near Auckland in 1873. It was almost certainly a copy of the scows used on North American Great Lakes. At this time there was a steady stream of settlers arriving from Canada who were quitting the harsh north environment to try their luck in warmer British lands. The early scows had leeboards, but these were soon discarded and centreboards fitted. By 1900 two scow types had evolved, the original Deck Scow which carried cargoes, often Kauri logs, on deck and the Hold Scow which had high hatches and carried cargoes below deck. They were fitted with one, two or sometimes even three centreboards and were all very shallow draught, about 3 ft (.90 m) light and only 6 ft (1.80 m) loaded. They had huge beams

There is a cloud of spray as a log is rolled off the New Zealand scow Rangi *at the Whangapara saw mill. The* Rangi *was built at Auckland in 1905 by the renowned scow builder George Niccol and was regarded as the best of her type built. She was 98 ft (29.40 m) long, 25 ft (7.50 m) beam but only drew 4 ft 8 in (1.40 m) of water (Alexander Turnbull Library, Wellington).*

and their general appearance was rather boxy but in spite of this they could work to windward and their flat bottom and shallow draught made them very fast running. Generally speaking they could hold their own with the normal ketches and schooners in the coastal and trans-Tasman trades.

The early scows were schooners, but by the 1890s the three-masted topsail schooner rig was being put into the large hulls. These large scows were trading regularly with timber across to Sydney and Melbourne and proved themselves capable deep water craft which could still load on an open beach. Also they were fitted with donkey boilers for steam winches which were used to handle the cargoes in and out.

The Tasmanian trading ketch Good Intent *of Hobart carries a sail plan typical of her type. She was regarded as being one of the best examples (State Library of South Australia).*

The Tasmanian Jane Moorhead *was built for trading but later operated in the crayfishery. Like the other Bass Strait fishing ketches she did not carry a jackyard topsail (State Library of South Australia).*

The 112 ft topsail schooner Huia was built in 1894 at Aratapu, New Zealand and under this sail plan set 5,700 sq ft (529.50 sq m) of sail. First in the New Zealand-Australia timber trade, she later spent thirty years in explosives trade between the two countries and was finally wrecked on a reef near Noumea, New Caledonia in 1951 (Danish Maritime Museum, Kronborg Castle).

OPPOSITE TOP

A hold scow racing at Auckland. The New Zealand style of lazy jacks can be seen, these made stowing the sail easier as it kept it gathered on the boom when the gaff was lowered. The water sail under the boom is just a race day addition (Alexander Turnbull Library, Wellington).

OPPOSITE BOTTOM

The firewood carrying scow Owhiti, built in 1925 was one of the last of her type (Clifford Hawkins).

CHAPTER FOUR

Coastal Craft

Sailing without an engine and continually being bashed by the wash of passing river traffic, we had quite a struggle in *Sea Fever* to make any progress against the tide to reach Rotterdam. Finally a river barge gave us a tow down to the Yacht Haven and we slid into berth beside a large and magnificent, if rather down at the heel, gaff cutter called *Hirta*. The rest of the sleek yachts of the Royal Mass Yacht Club clearly belonged to another and very different age. On being asked aboard we joined her cheerful young crew round a coal burning stove in the fo'c'sle. This 46 ft (13.80 m) pilot cutter, we learnt, had been built at Fowey in 1911 as the British Channel pilot cutter *Cornabra* and had originally been based at the Welsh coal port of Barry. Her crew had been lent the *Hirta* and were very proud of their recent fast North Sea crossing. The principle reason for this had been that the mainsail was so fragile with old age that they

The Truro River oyster boat George Glasson *has the peak of her main dropped so that the dredges remain on the bottom of the oyster banks in Carrick Roads, Cornwall. She has the straight stem and stern which suited the long Atlantic swell on the British West Coast (Author).*

The 42 ft (12.60 m) Alpha, *seen here running with a reefed square sail set, was not a typical Bristol Channel pilot cutter because in the competition to get the fastest cutter, pilots were going to builders all over Western Britain. The* Alpha *came in 1904 from a Fleetwood yard and closely resembled a Lancashire shrimping smack. She was given the name* Alpha *because her owner, Newport pilot William Prosser held licence number one. The* Alpha *proved fast and eventually Barry pilot Lewis Alexander discovered where she had been built and had the* Kindly Light *built at Fleetwood in 1911 (Author).*

dare not risk the strain of the reefing gear on it. The *Hirta* had ploughed through the sullen grey sea at great speed with her crew wondering what part of the gear would go first. They had been lucky, the most important gear had held and the *Hirta* had shot into the Hook of Holland more or less intact.

The pilot cutters from the Bristol Channel were one of the many types of coastal work boats which were suitable for conversion to yachts. The pilots operated independently and sailed out into the Bristol Channel 'seeking' ships bound into the ports they held a licence for. The pilots then boarded the ship and the two man crew sailed the cutter home which meant in effect, since one man was usually below resting, that they were sailed single handed for much of their time at sea. The cutters were intended to survive and be comfortable at sea in any weather and it was for this reason that so many became cruising yachts. The *Hirta* became a yacht in 1920 and was still making long cruises fifty years later as a training ship. Her owner at this time, Adam Bergius cruised her from the Clyde in 1970 with his wife and a crew whose average age was eleven! Over the years *Hirta* had had a considerable amount of work done on her but she was still very near to her original state and had the same mast, boom and gaff as in her working days.

The 37 ft (11.10 m) Amity *was a Great Yarmouth beach boat which took holiday makers on trips in the summer. It is believed that* Amity *was built by Chambers in 1912. Originally she would have been open but in 1916 she was sold to a Brancaster Staithe fisherman who had her decked in with a hatch and used her for collecting cockles and mussels. The Norfolk beach boat* Amity *is now a restored work boat sailed for pleasure (Author).*

Most pilot cutters were between 40-50 ft (12-15 m) long, but the largest cutter built was the 59 ft 2 in (17.75 m) *Mascotte*. Like so many working craft her design was strongly influenced by contemporary yachts. She was built in 1904 at Newport by pilot Thomas Henry Cox who employed the shipwright William Stacy to work with him. The *Mascotte* was fitted with rigging screws on the standing rigging instead of the usual deadeyes and lanyards. Pilot Cox held licences for both Barry and Newport but after 1913 when South Wales coal ports went over to steam cutters the *Mascotte* was sold as a yacht.

Because they had to compete in all weathers to reach a ship before their rivals, the pilots craft were usually the best for all round performances. The pilot cutters from the Bristol Channel and the slightly larger pilot cutters from the ports of Northern France were all noted for their ability to survive at sea in any weather and develop a reasonable turn of speed. The same qualities were found in the Dutch and German North Sea pilot schooners and the sleek schooners used by the American pilots. In Norway Colin Archer developed the traditional Scandinavian hull form into some rugged pilot cutters and 'rescue ships', lifeboats.

Inshore fishermen wanted craft which were easy to work in local wind and coastal

(Cont'd p. 64)

The Long Island Sound oyster and scallop dredging sloop Modesty *was built at Greenport, New York in 1923. With the trunk cabin she is a 'southsider' sloop which was recognised as being superior by Connecticut oystermen (John M. Kochiss).*

The Long Island Sound oyster sloop Nellie *has a single jib set on a boom which was the usual practice for American small craft (Author).*

A skipjack's jib being reefed. Like many American single headsails it is in lazyjacks (Author).

The pinkie Regina M *being repaired at Mystic Seaport Museum was the type of fishing schooner used in New England before dory carrying Gloucestermen became general in about 1860 (Author).*

The last Chesapeake Bay oyster sloop, J. T. Leonard *oyster dredging in 1965 (Chesapeake Bay Maritime Museum).*

In Holland members of the Society for the Preservation of the Botter have restored over 40 botters and about 30 similar fishing types back to their traditional working state. Large iron botters fished in the North Sea, but smaller inland sea ones like this one were all built of wood, mostly imported from Germany. The botters were known by their registration numbers but this one was given the name Windhaver *when sold for a yacht. She comes from the eastern shore of the Zuiderzee and was built at Harderwyh in about 1903 but at some stage was rebuilt with a stem typical of the Urk botters. In her working state she would have had a grapple anchor and in place of the cabin top she would have been open aft of the mast and had a fish well (Author).*

OPPOSITE TOP

The 52.16 ft (15.65 m) Friesland Skûtsje Fortuna, *built in 1917 is sailing here as a German yacht in the River Elbe. The Dutch flat and round bottom barges were superb working in their own narrow and shallow waterways and their tall narrow sails allowed them to sail very close to the wind, but at sea, compared to other European inshore craft they were generally difficult to get to windward in a seaway. It depended on the owner whether a curved or straight gaff was used, but a general rule was that the inland craft had round leeboards and the seagoing ones had long narrow leeboards (Author).*

OPPOSITE BOTTOM

The Dutch inland cargo craft had long, shallow draft, flat bottomed hulls. A widely used hull form was the round bowed, round sterned tjalk. There were many different types of tjalken and of these the ones used in Friesland were called Skûtsjes. The feeling for skûtsjes was so strong that after 1947 many towns in Friesland preserved a tjalk to take part in annual races on fresh water meers (Author).

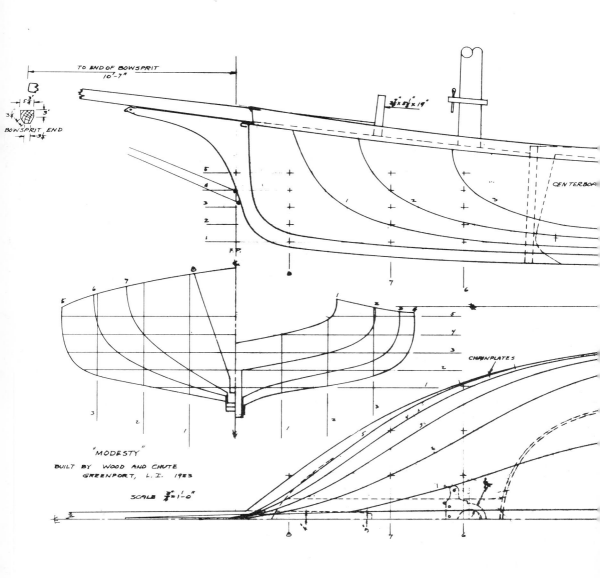

TO END OF BOWSPRIT
10'-7"

BOWSPRIT END

CENTERBOARD

CHAINPLATES

"MODESTY"
BUILT BY WOOD AND CHUTE
GREENPORT, L.I. 1923

SCALE ¾"=1'-0"

Modesty, *from Mystic Seaport Museum.*

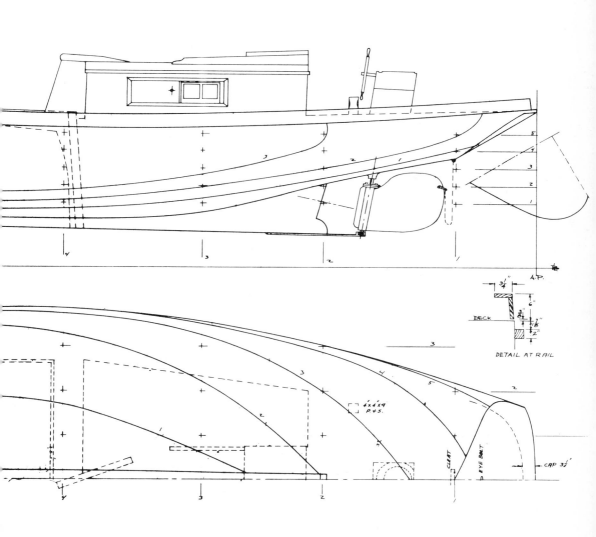

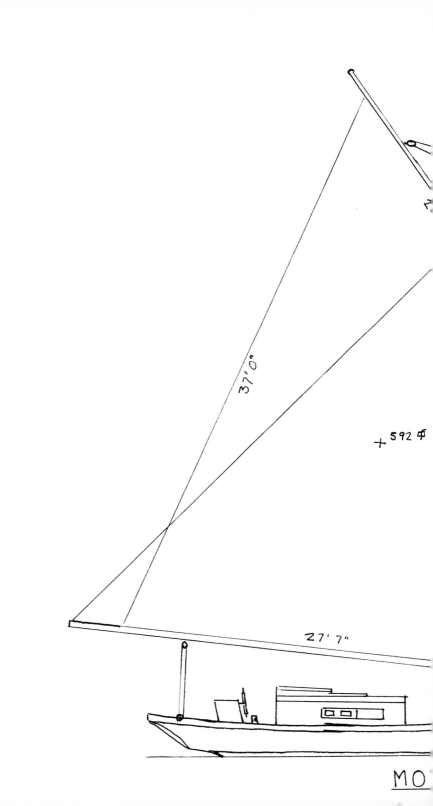

37'0"

+ 592 ∅

27' 7"

MO

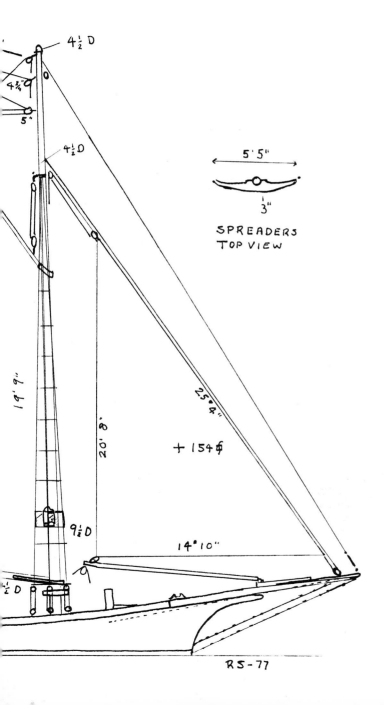

4½ D

4¾ D

5"

4½ D

5' 5"

3"

SPREADERS
TOP VIEW

19' 9"

20' 8'

25' 4"

+ 154 ☐

9½ D

14° 10"

½ D

RS-77

The steel 47 ft (14.10 m) Jenny III *was built at Antwerp in 1923 on the lines of Tholense hoogaars. The hoogaarsen and hengsten (which had blunter sloping bows) were the types of fishing vessels used in the Southern Netherlands, particularly on the River Schelde. In about 1900 the narrow stern of the Lemmeraak was introduced by builders into the Zeeland craft to make them faster so that strictly speaking later types should be called lemmerhoogaaren and lemmerhengsten (Author).*

conditions and this meant that virtually every port and village evolved its own purely local craft. At least that is the theory, but places with similar conditions never produced identical craft. National maritime customs and cultures played a very important part in producing a craft type. The craft used for oyster dredging in Britain were usually deep keeled cutters except the half decked transom sterned cutters on the South Coast, but across the North Sea in The Netherlands only a few hours sailing away, totally different craft were used such as the Tholense hoogaars which had flat bottoms, sloping flat bows, leeboards and tall masts with narrow gaff mainsails. On the Eastern Seaboard of the United States both English and Dutch influences were strong but a national maritime culture grew up which produced shallow draft centreboarders. Most of these were sloops, like the Long Island sloops *Priscilla,* built in Patchogue in 1888 and the *Modesty,* built 1923 which are both preserved by the Suffolk Maritime Museum, Sayville, Long Island. Other similar hull forms were the cat boats with single gaff sails on a mast right forward in the bow and the enormously beamy shallow draft sandbaggers and the narrow flat bottom centreboard sharpies.

Since the lemmeraak was the fastest of the Dutch traditional fishing boat types many yachts like the 34 ft (10.20 m) Saskia van Ryn *are still built to designs based on them (Author).*

Dixon Kemp stated that Captain Schank of the British Royal Navy invented the centreboard and built the first centreboarder in about 1774 at Boston, Massachusetts for Earl Percy. Captain Schank campaigned hard for the Royal Navy to adopt the centreboard, but an unsuccessful attempt with the *Lady Nelson* caused it to be abandoned. The centreboard was developed in the United States in work boats and yachts and it was not really until the 1870s that centreboards were accepted in Europe, and then only by yachtsmen. Work boat men deeply mistrusted the centreboard believing it would restrict the working space and weaken the hull.

However some European fishermen had by 1900 made some cautious experiments with centreboards. The fitting of centreboards into small open racing boats was steadily introduced after the 20 ft (6 m) American sloop *Truant* was brought to England in 1853 and beat all the crack 7 tonners on the Thames and went on to further success on the Mersey and Lake Windermere.

CHAPTER FIVE

Making Sail Work

The working gaff craft were often extremely picturesque but every feature of this design was purely functional. These working craft didn't have a mass of sophisticated machinery and general aids, they only had the skill and strength of the men on board to make use of the wind and tide to take them about their lawful business. Leaving harbour or a river was no problem for the small fishing craft because they could be rowed. Usually they lashed the tiller over one way and then rowed with heavy sweeps over the other side. To help them manoeuvre they often had a rowlock on the stern so that a sweep could be used to scull or just turn round a tight corner. When close tacking and the craft didn't have time to pick up speed a sweep was thrust down into the water over the windward quarter and the crafts stern levered so that the bow came up into the wind. The smaller schooners and ketches were too heavy to row except perhaps when drifting on the tide. In docks and small harbours warping posts were set up at every corner so that craft could be moved by horses or men hauling on ropes round the posts. If it was a shallow estuary then they were kedged out by using two anchors, one being recovered while the other was laid ahead by a man in a boat.

Another way of hauling craft to sea on its own windlass was to take a line to a fixed object ashore and then haul the craft forward. The best surviving example of this is at English Harbour, Antigua where the British men-of-war had to be hauled up the narrow twisting channel to reach this West Indian dockyard. I have seen the huge iron anchors still sunk into the rocky ground at strategic points so that the sailing ships could be hauled in and out. Also lining English Harbour are the great capstans which were once a common feature of every harbour. These could be used for warping, but really they were for careening, a method by which a vessel was hauled right over so that work could be carried out on one underwater side. Once a general practice, it survived in the tideless waters of the Baltic and the Caribbean much longer.

The ketch 'boomie' barges which once traded with coal into my home estuary of the River Deben had to go through the narrow channel over the bar first and then find their way up seven miles of twisting shallow estuary to Woodbridge. If they had a fair wind

OPPOSITE

The large Lowestoft smack Ena *has a 42 ft (12.60 m) beam trawl on her rail and a beautifully set main yard topsail. Many of these fine Lowestoft smacks were sold to Scandinavian owners and of these the 77 ft (23.10 m)* Excelsior, *built by Chambers at Lowestoft in 1921 was brought back for restoration in 1972. The* Jim Morgan, *built by Reynolds at Lowestoft in 1885, is a yacht in Sweden while the Göthenburgh scout training ketch* Leader *was built as a smack by Gibbs at Galmpton in 1892 (Jenkins).*

A Morecambe Bay nobby ashore at Fleetwood in about 1900 (Robert Shortall).

they sailed up but if there was no wind the crew had a back breaking job of towing the barge with a rowing boat with a line to the bowsprit end. When the wind was too strong or from the head then they stayed at anchor. Waiting for the right conditions was a large part of a sailors life. Often coastal ships lay days or weeks 'windbound' waiting for a favourable 'slant' of wind. Much of the work of keeping the sailing gear in reliable order was done during these monotonous periods at anchor in some sheltered bay or river.

All these ways of entering a port were supervised by a pilot or some local 'huffler' with good knowledge, but if the need arose every coastal ship master was expected to get his craft in unaided. The advent of the steam tug allowed such ships as the American multi-masted schooners to grow in size, but it seems to be forgotten that much of gaff seamanship was concerned with simply getting to sea. Even though the art of warping, kedging and controlled drifting on the tide were regularly practiced out of sheer necessity, it was still not as reliable as a powered craft. In estuaries trading craft were often put ashore because their crews and mud pilots didn't have the physical strength to control them on the tide stream all the time. When speaking with men who remembered the deeply loaded schooners sailing into Liverpool docks, they recalled how hard they often hit the dock walls if in a fierce tide the Captain slightly misjudged the entrance, yet many sailing wooden hulled vessels put up with this type of punishment for decades.

The conditions in sail were equally hard on the men and this came out in a discussion I had with some of the very few surviving Lowestoft smack skippers. On average they had started their working lives as cooks at thirteen, but in the case of one man whose family had been depressingly poor, he had been sent to sea at ten. The crew of five all lived down in the after cabin, but all the smacks were infested with fleas and rats. The

The Danish three masted topgallant schooner Jason *of Thuro has square sails set to get out of harbour (Danish Maritime Museum, Kronborg Castle).*

boys had to work with the men, but one of the cooks special tasks had been that when reefing he was thrown up into the sail and had to pass the reefing lace through the eyelets in the mainsail. Of course the loss of life in all the sailing fishing fleets was depressingly high.

The English trawling smacks from about 1870 were all ketches. Some of the finest ones built sailed from Lowestoft and Brixham. The Lowestoft smacks usually had round counter sterns and the main mast stepped well forward because this made the motion in the short North Sea seas better. Lowestoft smacks left their home grounds if fishing was poor and worked as far west as Padstow. In the English Channel they often landed fish on the open beach at Brighton, only going into Newhaven once a week to pick up coal and ice. The Brixham trawlers worked mostly in the long Atlantic swell so that they had their masts stepped well aft and had a deep forefoot on their keels. For trawling at night the Lowestoft men carried their lights in the mizzen rigging while the 'brickies' (Brixham) and Ramsgate smacks had their lights in the main rigging. Although one skipper told me all their lights were so poor that it was often impossible to see either.

At Lowestoft a watchman was paid to keep the boiler fire alight in harbour because without the aid of the steam capstan they could not get the mainsail up. Once clear of the harbour, the bowsprit was run out because the smacks would not handle properly

In Denmark careening was literally called keel hauling. Here the Matnilde, *built at Thuro in 1877 is hauled down for recaulking (Danish Maritime Museum, Kronborg Castle).*

until the jib was set. The actual trawling was done down wind on a whole six hour tide. The smacks only had to move just faster than the tide so that in a strong wind they often trawled under bare poles (no sails). After hauling the net with a capstan they sometimes got in another three hour 'drag' with the trawl if there was a weather going tide. Skipper Harry Genner once had the mainsail blown out on the *Godetia* and found that without it the smack simply would not sail. Even after he had sewn up the peak of the sail it took a week to get back to Lowestoft.

A few Lowestoft smacks like the *Sweet Home* and the *Golden Lily* set a 'flying jib' (jibtopsail), but like the mizzen topsail these sails were not considered much use. Most smacks carried a large 'tow foresail' which came past the main rigging. Brixham smacks set these on their annual races, but they were not normally thought to be worth bothering with. For the larger summer rig a yard topsail was very useful because in a calm this caught a draft aloft and kept the smack moving. However it required careful lowering because the yard could tear the mainsail or fall and kill someone working on the deck. In a strong wind the smacks had reefed mainsails, but kept the topsails set above them. This 'reef'n tops'l' rig kept the all important leading edge of the main area as long as possible. Not only did the powerful trawling ketches from Lowestoft and Brixham do this, but also the smaller Essex cutter smacks. The reef points on gaff sails usually extended half way up the luff, but some cruising yachts had an extra row from the third cringle across to the gaff jaw so that in a severe gale the gaff would be upright against the mast and just a small triangular sail area set.

The Norwegians also built ketches inspired by English trawlers. The Norwegian ketch had wide counter sterns because they often worked their fishing gear over the

Here on the Charlotte Rhodes *the anchor chain has been lifted from the pump action windlass so that the schooner can be hauled across a canal by a rope (Author).*

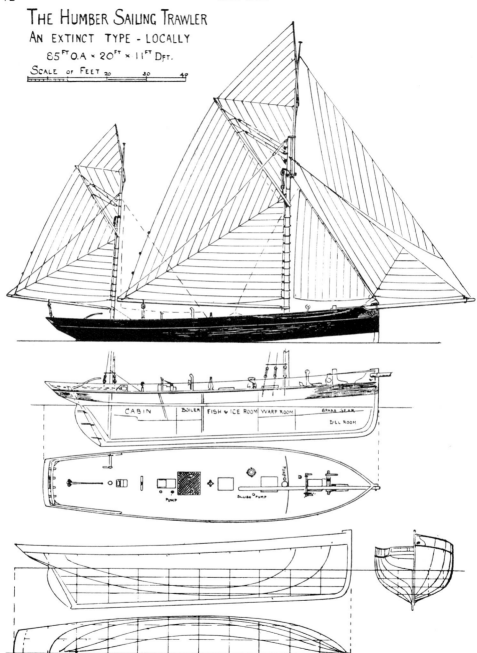

THE HUMBER SAILING TRAWLER
AN EXTINCT TYPE - LOCALLY
85 FT O.A × 20 FT × 11 FT DFT.
SCALE OF FEET 20   30   40

CABIN   BOILER FISH & ICE ROOM WARP ROOM   SPARE GEAR
                                                      DILL ROOM

PUMP   SLUSH PUMP

This Humber smack is typical of the English sailing trawlers. The ports of Hull and Grimsby were amongst the first to switch from sail to steam.

The galease Anna Møller *at Nyhavn, Copenhagen has the traditional deck galley which is just large enough for a man to get inside and do the cooking on a coal stove while wedged on a seat (Author).*

stern. To keep the stern free the sheet blocks were on chains and hooks so that they could be shifted about. On English smacks the lower halliard blocks were often on hooks so that they could be easily shifted about. All the running gear, although it required the strength of grown men to work, was very simple. The fishermen spent most of their time handling the nets and fish so that the actual sailing had to be left to one man most of the time. Very few working craft had running backstays and those that did had them well forward so that when beating to windward they were not touched. The strain with the gaff sail was from peak halliards pulling back and the gaff jaw pushing forward so that to keep the mast straight the forestays had to be kept tight.

Two completely different types of craft were used for fishing in the Thames Estuary, Rivers Colne and Blackwater and the Kent port of Whitstable. These had counter sterned smacks while Harwich, the Rivers Thames and Medway had transom sterned bawleys. The fishermen were often working beside each other and each swore that their type was the best. On balance it would seem the locally evolved bawleys were really more suitable for fishing while the Essex smacks probably only appeared because so many men from the Colne and Blackwater spent their summers as paid hands on yachts. The Essex cutter smacks were very similar to the Victorian cutter yachts which is hardly surprising since the Colne yards built both. Most Essex smacks carried a great deal of weather helm (a tendency to sail up into the wind) and for this reason they had long bowsprits and large jibs to try and offset this. These smacks often had very large mainsails but most of the time one reef was kept down. The extra sail was there, rather

The cargo winch on Anna Møller *and other fittings are traditional, but the derrick pole under the boom and the chain locker forward seem to be a modern addition (Author).*

like the bonnet on the foot of the Norfolk wherry's sail, only to be used in very light airs. In the winter the smacks went after shoals of sprats with stow nets. Since there was not room to use a drift net in the channels between the Thames Estuary sand banks the smacks and bawleys anchored and lowered the stow nets over the bow. With anchor and stow net down there was tremendous weight forward so that the 'stowboaters' all had powerful low set handspike windlasses. Also some smacks built to stowboat had a cut away forefoot and no rigging channels on the outside of the hull so that the fishing gear did not get fouled up. Since the winter weather was unpredictable the stowboaters put two reefs down in the mainsail so that they could make for shelter quickly. It was easier to shake a reef out than put one in.

When setting the loose footed mainsail the peak halliard was heaved up so tight that creases appeared in the sail just aft of the gaff jaw. This creasing was formed with no wind in the sail so that when the sail filled the shape came just aft of the mast while the leach became flat and like this the sail developed the best driving power. When beating to windward the mainsheet was kept eased a little and the smack not sailed too close to the wind therefore keeping the speed through the water fast. The sails on a gaff cutter will keep filled if the mainsheet is in really hard and the bows can be pointed higher into the wind, but often this results in a loss of speed and the craft just sliding sideways in the water. The great redeeming feature of the Essex smacks and similar cutters which sailed from King's Lynn and Boston into the narrow channels of The Wash was their ability to go to windward. This was largely achieved by stepping the masts well forward and having a very pointed bow which was kept as low as possible to reduce wind resistance.

The 35 ft (10.50 m) Wilhelm, *built in 1888 has an extremely beamy double ended hull with an 'outdoor' rudder which was a common feature of the Danish work boats. The original deck layout has been retained in this good restoration (Author).*

The Norwegian designer and boat builder Colin Archer, left, supervising the building of a sailing rescue ship, 1903 (Norwegian Folk Museum).

The building of the seventeenth century replica Nonsuch *at Appledore, England in 1968. The planks are being fastened with traditional wooden peg 'tren'als' (treenails) (Author).*

The building of the 91 ft (27.30 m) two masted centreboard wooden schooner John F. Leavitt *by Roy Wallace at Thomaston, Maine in 1976 (Author).*

Behind owner Ned Ackerman the frames of the John F Leavitt *are being shaped on the scrive board. This method was used in America, Newfoundland and Danish yards (Author).*

Caulking the new deck on the former British trading ketch Bessie Ellen, *under restoration at Troense, Denmark (Author).*

OPPOSITE
Built in 1904 of oak on oak and fastened with Swedish iron, most of L'Atalanta's *hull is still original, but like most other wooden hulls some of the covering board has had to be renewed (Author).*

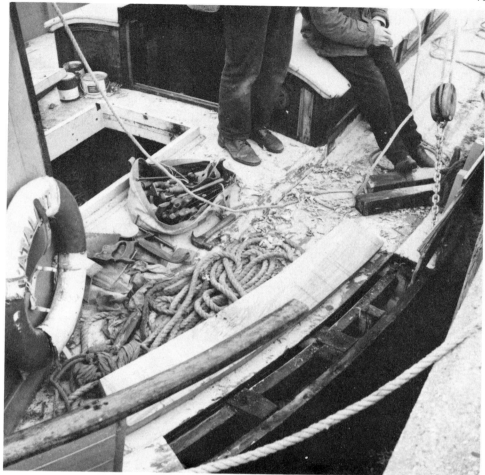

Most smacks lasted about 25 years, but a wooden hull will go on as long as it is kept water tight and any rot is renewed. In 1977 there were even a few Victorian wooden smacks working under power. There were the oyster dredgers *Our Boys* and *Puritan* at West Mersea which like the *Varuna* at Tollesbury had their topsides knarled with coats of tar applied over the decades. The former stowboater *My Alice* and the Whitstable *Thistle* were still working. The Whitstable 'yawls' were much more beamy and heavily built because they lay on moorings in the open sea and took the ground at low water. Most of the smacks still sailing for pleasure have at some time received a 'birthday' overhaul. The 33 ft (9.90 m) *Polly* was built with a transom stern by Howard at Maldon in 1892, but in 1919 she followed the fashion at Maldon by having a counter stern added and then in the mid 1970s she was largely rebuilt so that no one is certain how much of the original timber is left.

Some smacks have been converted to yachts like the 36 ft (10.80 m) long 5 ft (1.50 m) draft *Yet* built by Aldous in 1908 and oystering under sail until 1938 with a boom

The Anna Møller *is seen here in about 1916 as the trading galease* Esther, *built in 1906 (Danish Maritime Museum, Kronborg Castle).*

which went 4 ft (1.20 m) over the counter stern. The mainsail was made smaller when converted to a yacht but the topsail was added to keep the sail area about the same. A topmast backstay was also added but this is only set up when the jib topsail or the ghoster are set to prevent the topmast from being pulled forward. Other smacks have been restored back to their working state such as the *Gracie* which David Green rebuilt over a period of nine years at West Mersea. A marathon restoration was done by Ken Harris who bought a fire damaged 78 ft (23.40 m) Brixham trawler *Vigilance* and spent some seventeen years restoring her back to sail.

CHAPTER SIX

Sail Handling

In the early 1900s internal combustion engines started to be fitted to work boats. Over the following two decades they became effective enough to replace sail and as most of the deep draught sailing boat hulls were not suitable for power craft their owners were willing to sell them for conversion to cruising yachts. At the same period yachtsmen began to develop enormous admiration for the sea keeping qualities of certain working craft. In Britain the Bristol Channel pilot cutters and Brixham trawlers had a great influence on yacht design in the inter-war years. In the United States the New England and Gloucester fishing schooners had the same effect while in The Netherlands the flat bottomed inland waterway craft set the pattern for a whole new generation of Dutch barge yachts.

The blending of knowledge acquired by working men by trial and error and the requirements of cruising men produced some attractive yachts. The inspiration for the Nigel Warrington Smyth designed 38 ft (11.4 m) gaff cutter *Providence* came from Bristol Channel pilot cutters and the Brittany tunny fishermen. Built in 1934 the *Providence* was intended for deepwater cruising grounds in the English Channel so that the 7 ft (2.1 m) draught was no problem there. Although it has been rather a restriction while she has been based on the East Coast with its shallow channels and off lying sandbanks. The *Providence* and the better qualities of pilot cutters were a starting point when Laurent Giles designed the 46 ft (13.8 m) cutter *Dyarchy*, built in 1939. Her gear made use of modern material and yacht fittings so that *Dyarchy* is much more sophisticated than the Victorian cutters. Yet like the pilot cutters she could still be handled by two men. The same line of influence continued with the 46 ft (13.8 m) cutter *Corista*, built to J. Francis Jones design in 1952.

These large yachts were some of the finest gaff cruisers ever built, but they were going against the trend in yacht design because the bermudian triangular mainsail with a tall mast and closer windward ability was sweeping the board. The older heavy displacement boats still needed the extra sail area that the gaff gave them to push them through the water. Typical of this older generation of craft was the 49 ft (14.7 m) *Carlotta*, built at Gloucester by W. H. Halford in 1900 as a pilot cutter. She was unusual in having a clipper bow rather than the normal British straight stem. Apparently she was originally based at Barry, but later moved to Whitehaven under the name *Solway*. After conversion to a yacht she raced with the 12 metres on the East Coast and was then owned for thirteen years by Field Marshal Lord Gort. He kept her at East Cowes and actually preferred living aboard her than in his spacious castle, just above the moorings. World War II found her at St Peter Port, Guernsey owned by three partners. They left Guernsey one Sunday evening after church having heard that

The inland waterways of the East Anglian Broadlands produced unique local gaff craft. The cargo wherries with the sail hoisted by a single halliard originated from the open passenger rowed wherries once used on the Broads and the Thames. Two wherries are racing here at Wroxham in about 1902. The South River wherry, which did not have white on the bow, has a bow shaped like the eighteenth century rowing wherry. She must have been an old timer for her sail is squarer than later wherries and it is possible that she might have been spritsail originally (Author's Collection).

German officers had landed at the airport in the afternoon. The *Carlotta* was promptly becalmed about two miles outside, but later she made Fowey and then went on to Dumore East, but the Irish Republic would not allow her to stay and eventually she was laid up at Glasson Dock, Lancaster.

Here she was bought in 1942 by R. M. Twist who kept her for 27 years and for 17 of these years he lived aboard with his wife. They never made any long voyages, but cruised leisurely from island to island in Scotland, Ireland and Brittany. The *Carlotta* could run or reach in even the worst conditions. Dick Twist was never forced to heave to although in September 1950 in the North Channel a hurricane force wind over an ebb tide made the sea white all over and the *Carlotta* was laid down until the masthead truck was almost hitting the waves. Another time in the Sound of Bute a williwaw put her over until the water came up to the deck skylights.

The *Carlotta* drew 8 ft (2.4 m) of water and had 7 ton of lead on her keel and 3 ton of pig iron inside to make sure that she stayed upright. Given a good breeze she could make a fast passage. Some fast times Dick Twist made with her were from Wicklow Head in a N and NE wind to Longships in 24 hours and another time she was off the Manacles on the South Cornish coast at 7.15 am and was abeam the Abervrach lighthouse at 6 pm. This was under trysail in a strong NW wind. She was also sailed out of some tight corners, notably inside of Caladh Island in the Kyles of Bute as well as going south to north through the rocks inside the Raz de Sein. The *Carlotta* could not have stood up to the hard punishment of offshore cruising unless her gear had always been in good order. Her spars were her chief glory, all hollow oregon pine,

On the Norfolk wherry Zoe *a cabin top has been fitted over the cargo hatches to carry holiday makers. For summer sailing a bonnet has been added at the foot of the sail (John Perryman).*

A flourishing wherry and yacht hire industry was well established by the 1880s. The Broads inland yacht has the mast well forward for close wind sailing in the rivers (Jenkins).

except the solid topmast. From the deck to the truck was 60 ft (18 m) and 1,600 sq ft (149 sq m) of cotton sail was carried which was easily handled by Dick Twist and his wife.

When coming up to anchor the way was taken off her by letting the mainsheet out and backing the jib to stop her. In a crowded anchorage or small harbour where she had to be manoeuvred slowly, the jib was kept set and the mainsail halliards lowered at the same rate so that the peak still had a little drawing power. Normally the mainsail comes down easier if the throat halliard is eased first although with a loose footed sail it is possible to halve the area by hauling the luff up to the gaff jaw. When getting under way it is very important to top the boom up high with the topping lifts as it is virtually impossible to get the peak set well with the weight of the boom on the sail.

The argument, or perhaps it is more correct to call it pitched battle, over the best way to rig a sailing craft raged with surprising bitterness in the 1930s. It was a straight stand up fight between gaff and bermudian. Eventually there was an uneasy truce with it being agreed that bermudian was the best for racing and gaff was just right for cruising. However when I bought my first sizeable boat, the 28 ft (8.4 m) *Sea Fever* in 1957 I deliberately chose a gaff cutter. I was only interested in cruising and *Sea Fever*, a clinker hulled ex-ship's lifeboat with a centreboard, was the largest craft I could afford.

In the 1890s the inland yachts of the Norfolk Broads made a single jib more versatile by having a pole at the foot which was on a hinge on the mast and fixed to the bowsprit end by wire. For running, the wire was slackened so that the jib could be boomed out over the side (Jenkins).

She was heart breakingly slow to windward but reliable enough to usually get there in the end. Our first crossing of the North Sea under sail only took two and a half days to cover the 100 miles between the River Deben and Vlissingen (Flushing). My first foreign landfall gave me the same feeling of exaltation as Columbus must have felt when he hit the American Continent. That slow passage was no fault of the gaff sail, we simply had no lightweather sails and in the light summer's breezes *Sea Fever* could only creep over the gently rolling sea.

For 13 years I owned *Sea Fever* and sold her on buying the 35 ft (10.5 m) *L'Atalanta*. This is a very different gaff cutter, built of oak as the *Ran* on the West Coast of Sweden by Gustaffson at Landskrona for the Swedish customs service in 1904. Her lovely underwater hull has the deepkeel and beamy saucer shape so beloved by the Scandinavians, but when we first tried to sail her she was lifeless and at times sulked badly. As a working craft (of course without an engine) she would have had to go everywhere under sail. I decided to delve back into the past to discover the original sail plan. After much investigation facts began to emerge. The customs service had sold her in 1912 and the alterations really started when Salve Preisler of Malmö bought her. He was constantly altering her which included in 1926 making her one of the first

The 56 ft (16.80 m) Jolie Brise *was built as a Le Havre pilot cutter in 1913. She proved the offshore superiority of the work boat types over the yacht of the period by winning the Fastnet Race in 1925, 1929 and 1930 (Beken).*

On this 1930s racing yacht the jackyard topsail sheet has fouled up round the gaff end (Douglas Went).

yachts in Sweden to have a bermudian sail plan. The result was disappointing for although the gear was much lighter she would not sail at all well until the bowsprit and jib were put back. In 1933 Gunner Malmquist bought her for a voyage round the world. Whether he ever made this there is no way of telling, but *L'Atalanta* reverted back to being a gaff cutter, acquired a wheelhouse and eventually appeared on the British register.

By the time I acquired this black cutter she had had at least six different name changes and nine different owners. There was a clear pattern through almost seventy years. Firstly she was an attractive homely old craft which encouraged successive owners to look after her, but as the engine size increased the sails became less important and replacements had been ordered without too much concern to their effectiveness. It was not possible to find the exact original sail plan so instead there were long discussions with Jim Lawrence, a sailmaker who specialises in traditional craft sails. One idea was to give her the same sail plan as an Essex smack, but I wanted to keep as near to the original rig as possible. The pole mast was a starting point. Although this British Columbian Pine spar had been made in about 1947 it was the same measurements as the one she had had when she came from Sweden and the sail plan was designed to fit the existing spars.

On *Sea Fever* the mainsail was laced to the boom and there was Turner roller reefing gear. Using roller reefing at sea in a strong breeze usually resulted in creases appearing in the sail as it was rolled down. The final stage of the pilot cutters in the Bristol

A Danish custom cutter in about 1900 with full crew (Troense Museum).

The Sea Fever *running with every possible sail set, including a watersail under the boom, during the 1968 East Coast Old Gaffers Race (Yachting Monthly).*

L'Atalanta *at this stage needed the mainsail foot altered so that it came down below the boom and the topsail recut. The light weather foresail was originally intended to fill the fore triangle on* **Sea Fever** *(Author).*

Channel had Appledore roller reefing gear and it was a considerable safety factor. *L'Atalanta's* mainsail is loose footed and a new one was made without much alteration to the total sail area, but the gaff was peaked higher. Three foot was sawn off the end of the gaff as the former sail area so far aft was producing weather helm rather than forward thrust. This new loosefooted mainsail is a really powerful and handy sail. By hardening the outhaul at the after boom end the sail can be made flat while going to windward and by freeing the outhaul it has a 'belly' for running. The reef points, beautifully traditional, never the less really do make reducing sail more of a problem and are slower than roller reefing. To tie the aft-most points often means standing on a wet slippery deck with both hands in the air. In the early nineteenth century the 200 ton Leith passenger smacks which raced between London and the Scottish ports actually had footropes on the boom so that the seamen could go out to the end when reefing. Even so in the age of working sail an awful lot of good men were thrown into the sea while reefing gaff sails.

Although man-made ropes are used for much of the running rigging nothing but canvas would look right for the mainsail area on a craft of such obvious strong character. The main and foresails were made up in Gourock RN flax No 4 while the jib

On L'Atalanta, *the author, Pearl Simper and Bill Coke (Hugh Perks).*

is in 12 oz (341 gm) American cotton in 18 in (458 mm) panels. An increase in the size of the jib instantly gave *L'Atalanta* more balance under sail. The jib was altered back to one set flying, rather than hanked to a stay, because lowering is so much easier if the traveller is let go as the halliard is released allowing the sail to come down on the leeward deck. Most of the larger gaff craft solve the problem of keeping the jib luff taut (so that they can sail closer to the wind) by having a gun tackle on one end of the halliard.

The overall effect of the revised sail plan gave *L'Atalanta* enough extra speed to make her once again manoeuvre under sail. Even in this age of packed anchorages it is still personally satisfying to pick up a mooring and beat into harbours, when ever practical, under sail. Yet the diesel engine is the one modern 'improvement' which has not been thrown out. The 23 in (585 mm) propeller and weight of the engine undoubtedly spoils her sailing abilities and the wheelshelter, a curious structure which is in fact the front of Gunner Malmquist's wheelhouse, must create windage which further slows her down, but it is highly practical in bad weather so that it has been kept.

Since the revised sail plan has been made I have seen sail plans of very similar Scandinavian customs cutters of 1890. We hadn't increased the sail area enough, the boom should have gone several feet out over the stern. However for our coastal passage making with my youthful family usually as the crew there is as much sail as we can manage. The Customs men would have wanted more sail to keep them moving in light airs. For this we have a yard topsail which requires great patience to get aloft and it has

The former pilot cutter Carlotta *in the Odet River leaving Saint Marine in Brittany (R. M. Twist).*

been known to resist being hauled down again. One of *L'Atalanta's* most spectacular sails was once when running down the Swin Channel towards the River Thames. The wind started to freshen and the topsail was left set too long and became pinned to the peak halliards. The wind continued to freshen so that by the time we had reached the mouth of the Thames *L'Atalanta* was ploughing through the water and pushing up a huge white bow wave. To ease the strain aloft and on the hull I would like to have come up into the wind and got the topsail down but by then the wind over the ebb had pushed up an angry chop and with Sea Reach and Lower Hope full of huge commercial shipping coming down on the tide there really was not enough safe room to wallow about in the main channel. Eventually, under the lee of a cruise liner at Tilbury the pressure on the topsail eased and it came down.

Really a yard topsail on a pole mast is only effective when running or reaching. To make a topsail work properly a topmast is needed. For going to windward we have found a light ghoster jib, which virtually fills in the foretriangle, the best. Usually this type of headsail is cut rather baggy just for running and reaching but since *L'Atalanta's* weakest point of sailing is going to windward she needed a flat cut ghoster. In order to keep pointing up into the wind a craft needs to be sailing fast through the water. Under normal working headsails the routine for going about is to release the jib sheet as soon

Ropes, Spars and Sails of a Cutter, Yawl and Schooner.

CUTTER'S SPARS and ROPES.

1	Lower mast and hoops.		22	Fore halliards.
2	Topmast.		23	Jib sheets.
3	Bowsprit.		24	Fore sheet,
4	Main boom.		25	Bowsprit shrouds.
5	Gaff.		26	Whiskers.
6	Topsail yard.		27	Jib topsail sheet.
7	Spinnaker boom.		28	Spinnaker boom topping lift.
8	Tiller.		29	Spinnaker boom brace.
9	Shrouds.		30	Maintopmast backstay.
10	Topmast shrouds.		31	Reef pennant.
11	Crosstrees.		32	Main outhaul.
12	Peak halliards.		33	Gaff topsail clew line.
13	Throat or Main halliards.		34	Gaff topsail sheet.
14	Boom topping lift.		35	Jib topsail halliards.
15	Runners and tackles.		36	Burgee.
16	Forestay.		37	Gaff topsail halliards.
17	Topmast stay.		38	Channels.
18	Bobstay.		39	Main sheet.
19	Bobstay fall.		40	Fore sheet.
20	Jib traveller.		41	Spinnaker boom guy.
21	Jib halliards.		42	Ensign.

CUTTER'S SAILS, &c.

A	Mainsail.	E	Jib topsail.	H	Forecastle.
B	Foresail. C. Jib.	F	The quarter.	I	Stem, Cutwater.
D	Gaff topsail.	G	Midships.	K	Truck.

YAWL'S MIZEN.

A	The sail, or mizen.	4	Main yard.	8	Mizen halliards.
1	Mast.	5	Stays.	9	Mizen sheet.
2	Bumpkin.	6	Brails.	10	Bumpkin shrouds.
3	Mizen boom.	7	Shrouds.	11	Mizen tack.

SCHOONER'S SPARS and ROPES.

1	Mainmast.		23	Jib sheet.
2	Foremast.		24	Bobstay.
3	Bowsprit.		25	Fore peak halliards.
4	Main boom.		26	Main peak halliards.
5	Maintopmast.		27	Main throat halliards.
6	Foretopmast.		28	Fore throat halliards.
7	Main gaff.		29	Forestaysail sheet.
8	Fore gaff.		30	Fore crosstrees.
9	Maintopsail yard.		31	Main crosstrees.
10	Foretopsail yard.		32	Jib halliards.
11	Squaresail boom.		33	Jib traveller.
12	Main topping lifts.		34	Triatic stay.
13	Squaresail yard lifts.		35	Maintopmast stay.
14	Squaresail yard guys.		36	Main gaff topsail tack.
15	Squaresail yard brace.		37	Fore channels.
16	Davit falls.		38	Main channels.
17	Davits.		39	Tiller.
18	Main shrouds.		40	Main sheet.
19	Fore shrouds.		41	Reef pennant.
20	Forestay.		42	Reef cringles.
21	Bowsprit shrouds.		43	Maintopsail sheet.
22	Foretopmast stay.			

SCHOONER'S SAILS, &c.

A	Mainsail.	D	Jib.	G	
B	Foresail.	E	Maintopsail.	H	} Reef points.
C	Fore staysail.	F	Foretopsail.	I	

NOTE.—*In sails, the lower four corners are called the tacks, and the after corners the clews ; of the sides, the upper part is the head; the lower the foot; the fore part the luff ; the after part the leach.*

The technical terms used on British gaff yachts in the 1890s and sail plans on opposite page.

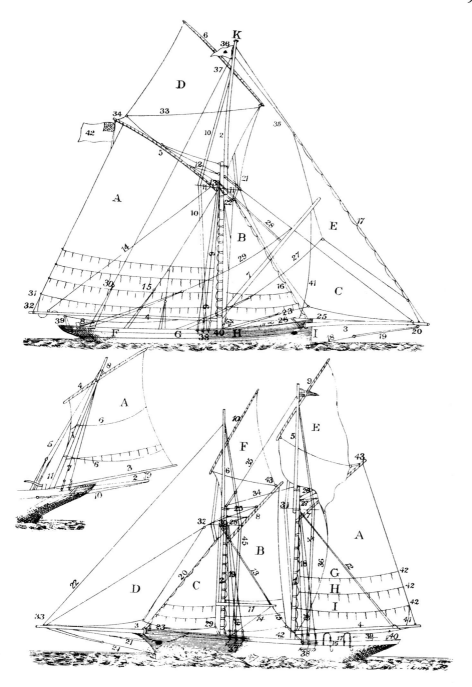

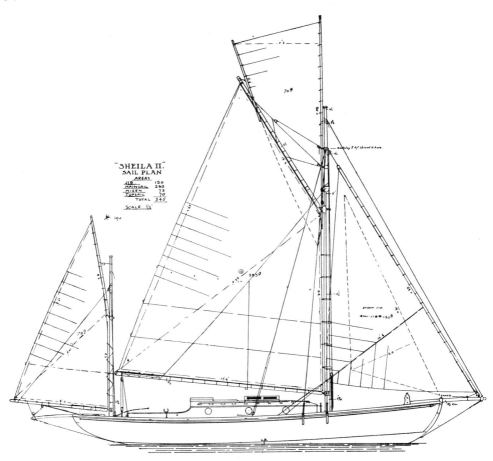

The 31 ft (9.30 m) British cruising yacht Sheila II *built in 1910 has a single headsail. Judging by the performance of another canoe-sterned yawl, the 30 ft (9 m)* Nereid II *built to G. U. Law's design in 1913, this is a good hull and sail plan combination.*

as the helm is put down. This releases the weight forward and lets the craft's head come up into the wind. By this time the craft is losing way so that both jib and foresail are briefly abacked to make sure she comes round on to a fresh board. Going about with the huge ghoster means the sail quickly wraps itself round the forestay and any member of the crew trying to handle it round. Jim Lawrence's answer to this was a brail which when going about hauls most of the sail up to its luff and then is released to let it down the other side of the forestay.

A large headsail is only for beating in light airs. Keeping the large headsail set when beating to windward in a fresh breeze can give the impression of speed by laying the craft over well. Really it is very difficult to get the sheet in bar tight and it is more likely that one starts to sail slightly off the wind. Sometimes one is even forced off the wind by the sail pressure forward. The Essex smacks seem to go to windward well with their low

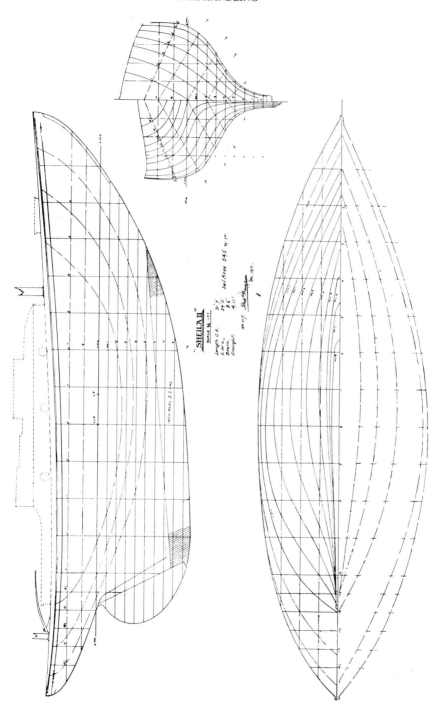

"SHEILA II"
SCALE ¼ in.
Length O.A.   37.7'
L.W.L.   27.0'
Beam   8.6'
Draught   4.11'
Nº 117   Alfred Mylne
Sail Area 545 sq. ft.
Dis. 10 T.

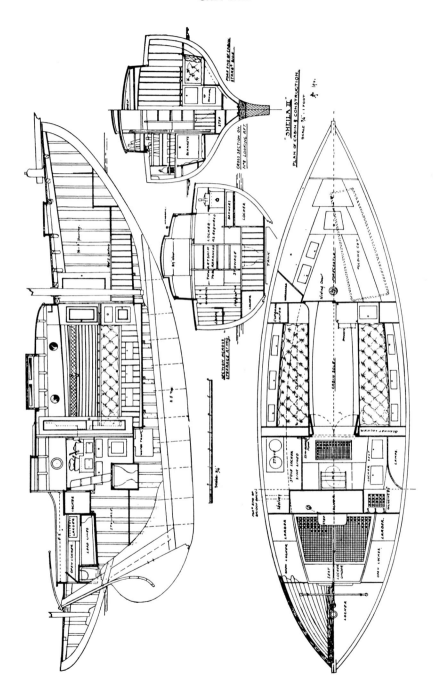

"SHEILA II"
PLAN OF CABIN & CONSTRUCTION
SCALE ¾″: 1 FOOT

Charlie Stock's Shoal Waters *was originally rigged in 1963 with gear switched from his previous 16 footer, the gunter rigged* Zephyr, *in which he had been cruising single handed since 1948.* Shoal Waters *now carries 170 sq ft (15.79 sq m) of sail and 280 lbs (127.12 kg) ballast. Charlie regards the furling gear, by which the headsail can be rolled up without leaving the cockpit, to be the most important improvement (Author).*

An English East Coast scene with the gaffer Providence, *barge* Reminder *and steam puffer* Vic *(Author).*

The 35ft (10.50 m) long, 13 ft (3.90 m) beam Norwegian prawner Boan *was built of pine at Risor in 1927. Bought by an Englishman in 1969 she is seen here being rigged at Peldon, Essex (Author).*

The gaff cutter Corista *has the traditional rigging channels outside the hull, but her tall narrow sail plan is really the new generation gaff (Author's Collection).*

cut jibs set on a long bowsprit with the sheets belayed forward in the eyes of the craft.

I hardly dare admit, after all that talk about keeping her traditional, but our ghoster is of a man-made fibre. Very slippery to handle, but it does combine a light weight cloth with maximum strength. When *L'Atalanta's* standing rigging was renewed it was kept to hand spliced plough share wire which combined traditional appearance with practical requirements since her last set had apparently lasted about 35 years. At the same time some mast hoops were renewed, none were being made in Britain so that replacements came from Svendborg, Denmark. The British masthoops are riveted together while the Danish ones have bolts which make them easier to fit but the nutheads can cause the hoops to jam together when the sail is being hoisted.

I have just mentioned some of the lessons we have learnt. Every craft behaves slightly differently so that one just has to keep trying until all her little habits have been discovered.

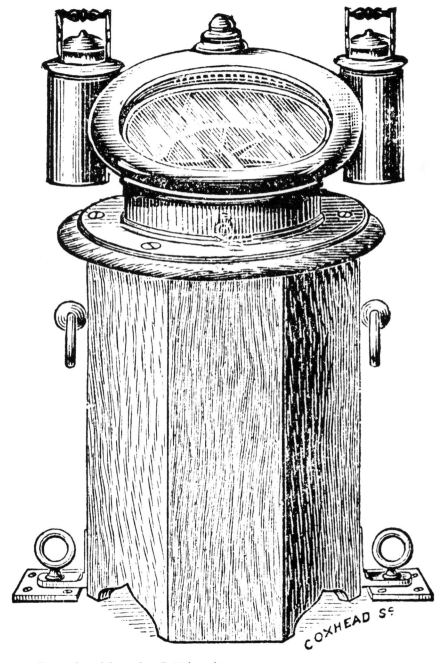

The type of binnacle widely used on British yachts.

CHAPTER SEVEN

Ocean Wanderers

There is no set pattern to which people who make long voyages under sail conform. Every craft is slightly different and so too is the way that people make their cruises, very much depends on their personal wishes, physical stamina and financial state. One thing is certain, the gaff sails carried a great many in perfect safety across the oceans of the world.

Although the sea itself has not changed the type of cruising has. A typical old style cruise was made by the schooner *Halcyon* as the dust of World War I was settling down and yachting slipped back into its previous elegant style for a few more seasons. Between December 1921 and April 1922 she made a Mediterranean cruise down the West Coast of Italy to Sicily. From here she crossed to Greece so that the nine guests in the owners party could visit the classical ruins and finally they turned up the Adriatic to Venice. None of the guests took any part in working the schooner; all this was left to the professional skipper, five paid hands and a maid.

A very different style of voyaging was adopted by Peter and Anne Pye after World War II. In 1934 they had bought the 29 ft (8.70 m) Looe fishing lugger *Lily*, built in 1896 and converted her to the auxiliary gaff cutter *Moonraker*. Over the following summers they managed to sail from England up the River Seine, to Holland, Denmark and just into the Baltic. In 1946 they visited the south west of Ireland and Spain the following year. This was about as far as could be reached in a summer holiday. In the turmoil of post-war Britain the National Health Service emerged and this held no appeal for Doctor Pye, so with his wife he decided to live on *Moonraker* and make a series of long cruises. Between cruises Peter Pye wrote three books and gave lecture tours so that the *Moonraker* became well known to a whole generation of sailing people.

The Pyes delighted in visiting lonely places and out of the way islands. Their first voyage was to the West Indies and back, but the next was even more ambitious as it took them into the Pacific to Galapagos and Society Islands, Honolulu, British Columbia and Alaska, before they explored Central America. Then followed a visit to Finland and finally a lengthy voyage to Brazil.

Another Cornish lugger to make a long voyage was the 34 ft (10.20 m) *Lucent*. She was converted to a yacht in 1926 and in the mid 1960s Roger Jameson and David Balfour made a leisurely six year voyage from England across the Pacific to Sydney. They reckoned that the ketch was a single hander as one man on deck could handle her while the other slept. The voyage to Sydney was mostly 'down hill' sailing, in fact, on the actual passages from Falmouth to Fiji she was only tacked in earnest six times.

The conversion of working craft to yachts reached almost epidemic proportions in the inter-war years. In 1936 Christopher St J. Ellis had the Leigh bawley *Elsie Mildred*,

The schooner Halcyon *passing Mount Parnassus during a Mediterranean cruise in 1921. For this winter passage the large mainsail has been left stowed and a smaller trysail set above it (Author's Collection).*

The trysail sheets on the stern of the Halcyon *(Author's Collection).*

The maid on the Halcyon *(Author's Collection).*

The 28 ft (8.40 m) Peirson *was built in 1869 at St Helier, Jersey. She has a pole mast very similar to work boats found on the other side of the English Channel between The Solent and Cornwall. In her early days in the Channel Islands she was used for smuggling, but later became a racing yacht. In 1940 she was one of fifteen craft from St Helier Yacht Club which took part in the evacuation of British troops from St Malo. Later she took escaping Islanders across to England and was finally abandoned in the River Dart (Author's Collection).*

which had been built in 1901, converted to a yacht. The bawley had a handspike windlass with heavy anchor chain stowed on the deck. This had been all right for fishing in the Thames Estuary, but in the open sea the chain was washed all over the place and was a great problem. The *Elsie Mildred* needed several headsails set to counteract the weather helm, but she often overtook yachts when reaching in a strong breeze.

This bawley was taken to the Netherlands and into the Ijsselmeer, but the last trip was through the Forth & Clyde canal to Gare Loch where she won the Public School race. She was continuing the trip round Britain when World War II was declared and she had to be left at Castletown, Isle of Man. Eventually she was broken up here. After World War II Chris Ellis borrowed the pilot cutter *Cariad* and after fitting out at Pin Mill cruised to Norway with a crew of schoolboys. This really started off a series of annual cruises which eventually grew into the Ocean Youth Club. Chris Ellis bought the 53 ft (15.90 m) *Theodora* next which had started life as a pilot cutter the *Kindly Light*. The pilot cutters enjoyed such popularity because compared to the gaff yachts of the same size they were easier to maintain and sail. The *Theodora* was later loaned to

OPPOSITE:
Peter and Anne Pye's cutter Moonraker *in British Columbia (Mrs Anne Pye).*

The former pilot cutter Theodora *off Cape Cod in 1958. The yard had been added so that she could set square sails when running before the Trade Winds (C. St J. Ellis).*

The bawley Elsie Mildred *was converted to a yacht by adding a gaff and boom mainsail and a cabin top, but she still had a hand spike windlass (C. St J. Ellis).*

A clipper bowed yawl at Tayvallich, a land loched anchorage on Loch Sween on the Scottish West Coast, about 1936 (Gilchrist — Author's Collection).

The Mjojo *at the start of the East Coast Old Gaffers Race in 1970 when in gale force winds she was one of five boats to finish out of seventeen starters out of an entry of eighty (Author).*

The 38 ft (11.40 m) cutter Golden Vanity *was built at Galmpton in 1908 as a 'nice little single hander' for marine artist Arthur Briscoe. She is seen here at the start of the 1972 Single-handed Trans Atlantic Race when Peter Crowther took eighty-eight days to reach America. In all he made four Atlantic crossings in* Golden Vanity *and the best was eighteen days from the Canary Islands to the West Indies. He found her a fantastic boat, but after covering 25,000 miles in three years, including being stranded on a reef off St Croix where she half filled with water, she needed a major refit and he sold her (Author's Collection).*

the Ocean Youth Club in the late 1960s but they began to regard her as a huge floating maintenance problem. The countless hours of skilled work needed to keep her fit to meet all weather just seemed pointless when compared to a plastic hulled yacht. The club aimed to get young people to sea and were not trying to preserve an old craft, even though she was obviously an important part of Britain's maritime heritage. The *Theodora* was taken over by the Maritime Trust, while the Ocean Youth Club built a fleet of powerful modern cruising ketches but they kept the 50 ft (15 m) Edwardian gaff yawl *Duet*.

Many people still believe that the gaff sail is the most handy for a cruising yacht. Rod Pickering designed the 42 ft (12.60 m) *Mjojo* with a gaff cutter rig which included a loose footed mainsail. The *Mjojo* was built by local craftsmen on the beach at Lamu in Kenya. The hull was left bare wood and just oiled but was coated with fibreglass below the waterline, and only the attractive Arabic carvings were picked out in bright colours. She left Lamu in July 1967, went to the Seychelles, Durban then round the Cape of Good Hope to the lonely isle of St Helena and across to Rio de Janeiro. In April 1970 she left here and cruised via Salvador and the Azores to Falmouth and then to the Thames Estuary. That year she took part in the East Coast Old Gaffers Race sailing in gale force winds and was one of only five boats to get round the course.

The Maresca, *built by Luke at Hamble in 1906 was a Southampton day boat later adapted for cruising (John Clarke).*

In late October, 1965 the Maresca *left the Hamble for a final sail of the season, but while returning from Ryde pier she grounded on the Rainbow bar off Titchfield Haven. Due to the loss of her kedge anchor she could not be got off in the increasing wind and she pounded so badly on the sand that the caulking worked lose and* Maresca *sank and later broke up (John Clarke).*

A staunch believer in the practical assets of the gaff sail is Charles Stock who bases his 17 ft (5.10 m) *Shoal Waters* at Heybridge in Essex. The *Shoal Waters* has no engine, but has visited, usually single handed, most of the English coast between Yorkshire and the Isle of Wight as well as across to Belgium. On average this 17 ft cutter covers about 1,300 miles a year. Between 1963, when he bought the moulded Fairey Falcon hull, and 1977 the *Shoal Waters* has covered 18,000 miles. Much of this achievement is due to Charlie Stock's good seamanship, but his cruises have shown how a modern light weight hull with a gaff rig can make a very successful cruiser.

CHAPTER EIGHT

Racing

The love of competition is a deep rooted part of man's basic instincts and testing ones ability afloat racing, is a superb outlet for this need. When yacht racing began the owners bet on their craft beating all rivals and this progressed into an organised sport. In Britain racing really began on the River Thames, but when this mighty tideway became too overcrowded with commercial shipping the gentlemen yachtsmen boarded the new railway trains and travelled down to the South Coast where they made Cowes the mecca of yachting. In this really grand yachting, huge yachts crewed by professional paid hands spent the summer going around the coastal regattas racing for cash prizes. Until about 1870 racing yachts tended to be simply finer lined versions of cruising yachts largely because their owners lived aboard and needed the space. However, racing yachts gradually developed into a separate type of craft designed purely for speed with no consideration for the comfort of those living aboard.

Racing a yacht was rather like racing a horse. The owner would often follow the event in a steam yacht and his main function was to pay the expenses. Some owners went a step further and also had small steam launches for towing the racing yachts. For instance the steam screw schooner *Amazon* (now being restored by the actor Arthur Lowe) was built to act as a tender to Tankerville Chamberlayne's huge racing cutter *Arrow*.

Racing brought many improvements to yachts which in turn were then adapted for cruising yachts and work boats. Only the wealthy yacht owners had the money to experiment with new designs, but in order to make racing fair and put everyone on an equal footing, handicapping and rules were introduced. This meant that designers now started to produce yachts which were able to receive good handicap and consequently win on rating rather than be the first round the course. In Britain this resulted in the narrow plank-on-edge hull type. A highly successful racer of this type was the 46 ft (13.80 m) cutter *Madge* whose greatest beam was 7 ft 9 in (2.32 m). She was designed by G. L. Watson and built at Govan just outside Glasgow in 1879. In her first two seasons racing around Britain she was a constant prize winner but by then she was 'out built' under the RYA tonnage rule. She was sold to the United States in 1881 and had more success in the regattas on the Eastern Seaboard.

Racing forced the development of deep narrow hulls in Britain while in the United States it pushed the shallow, beamy hulls to extremes. In both cases racing handicap systems went too far and caused yacht design to take the wrong turning and produced craft which were basically unseaworthy. The British plank-on-edge types needed so much ballast that they were known as 'lead mines' and were very wet at sea while some American schooners attempted to carry so much sail on shallow hulls that they

(Cont'd. p. 120)

In the 1890s racing yachts found that a higher peaked mainsail improved their windward ability but it robbed them of a decent sizable topsail for running. The answer seen here on the schooner Cirely *was the jackyard topsail above her mainsail (Author's Collection).*

The Edwardian cutter Moya *racing at Cowes. The strain of the mainsail through the peak halliards and gaff jaw has pulled the top of the mast back (Author's Collection).*

The 52 ft (15.60 m) cutter Penitent *racing on the Clyde in 1898 (Author's Collection).*

One-design classes were introduced so that more people could take part in racing. Here are the
Solent One Designs Eilun Toto *and* Margaret *racing. Started in 1895 this was the first organised*
one-design racing class in Britain (Author's Collection).

The Seabird Half Rater one-design class racing at Treaddur Bay, Anglesey. The 20 ft (6 m)
gunter rigged Seabirds class was started in 1898 and is now the oldest class racing regularly in
Britain (Seabird Association).

Bristol Channel pilot cutters racing in 1906. Each is carrying a massive sail area and all have the original form of spinnaker boomed out also some have a watersail (usually an old jib) under this and the main. Three cutters have spars extending from the main boom with an extra sail hoisted from the gaff end (National Museum of Wales).

Start of the Little Ship's Club's Brightlingsea-Ostend Race in 1930 with Curlew *leading* Ilex *(D. Went).*

The Osprey *at the start of a race in the River Colne. In the 1930s gaff boats dropped out of serious racing because their large sail area was a considerable disadvantage in the handicap system (D. Went).*

Before the coming of the railways, smacks used to sail to Billingsgate Fish Market, London for the traditional opening of the season's oyster market. The Whitstable Stormy Petrel *is making ready to take part in the first annual Thames Oyster Smack Race in 1972 which was begun as a revival of the old custom (Author).*

The clipper bowed Panther *racing on the Clyde in about 1935 (Gilchrist — Author's Collection).*

The Alando *in the 1974 East Coast Old Gaffers Race. The Old Gaffers Races are held all round the coast of Britain and in North France as day events (Author).*

The schooner Golden Hind *and the yawl* Fedoa *at the start of a race on the Clyde in about 1933. (Gilchrist — Author's Collection).*

Judge Blagdon's Alando *and the* Biddy, *built by Howard at Maldon in 1906, taking part in the Pin Mill Sailing Club race on the River Orwell in about 1938. Both craft have sweeps in the usual place in racks on the rail, as rowing home was often more reliable than the temperamental marine engines of that period (D. Went).*

The gaff cutter Minoru *on the Clyde in about 1935 (Gilchrist — Author's Collection).*

capsized. The real drawback was that cruising yacht designers tended to follow the current racing fashions.

The ultimate in gaff racers was reached before World War I with fine lined hulls with vast spreads of canvas including jackyard topsails and numerous headsails but these dropped out of serious racing in the 1920s. When the Old Gaffers Association events revived interest in competitive gaff sailing this was really a return to a much more informal style. The Old Gaffers Races and the various work boat events are as much rallies as anything else and most of the craft taking part are fitted out for cruising. The true Edwardian racing yachts have long since gone and most of the survivors of that era are small open day racers, which because of the RYA handicap system usually come out as some of the major prize winners in the Old Gaffers events.

CHAPTER NINE

Gaff Revival

It is a basic need of humanity to discover and come to terms with its own past. In most of the developed industrial nations this need produces a fascination with sailing craft of the past because they worked perfectly capably aided only by the elements. There is also the desire to preserve everything connected with traditionally evolved sailing craft. It is perfectly logical that the North Eastern seaboard of the United States and England should have seen more sailing craft preserved than anywhere else because their past were so shaped by them. The Netherlands and Denmark also have a strong appreciation of their national types of sailing craft and although not quite so widely spread the same feelings are found in many other western nations, particularly Canada, Australia, France and Germany.

The revival of gaff sail is part of this world wide upsurge of interest in classic sailing craft. Certainly the renewed interest has been greatly fanned by the successes of the Old Gaffers Races. The first Old Gaffers Race took place on the Hamble in 1958 and was simply to settle an argument between three owners as to who owned the fastest boat. In 1963 another Old Gaffers Race was started on the East Coast and the original course was from Osea Island to Harwich. There was much nail biting as to whether any boats would turn up to such an event. Some thirty boats turned up at the starting line, but a virtual flat calm saw them drifting down river on the tide. With *Sea Fever* we went ahead of the racing fleet into Harwich, only to our embarrassment to receive the winning gun. There was worse to follow when going ashore, for at the Pier Hotel, supper was ready for all the crews and not a gaff boat in sight until the real leader *Corista* sailed swiftly into Harwich in the moonlight. Looking back one can see that the gaff revival dates from around this period, but at the time it seemed like total disaster. The Old Gaffers Races received very wide coverage in national and local press and over the next few years brought respectability and topsails back to the gaff rig. Both races took a few years to get the bugs out of the system. The South Coast Race really got going when it moved to Cowes and the East Coast Race did the same when the Stone Yacht Club took it under its wing and the course was made more feasible by going from the River Blackwater out to sea and back. Of the 1966 race I wrote in *Sea Breezes* 'the sight of forty old yachts and smacks . . . all beating at sea up to the Priory Spit buoy convinced me that traditional sail is far from being dead and is in fact experiencing a form of revival'.

These races made an impact on the whole boating scene and ended the period of isolation for the gaff boat. It was noticeable that after the mid 1960s gaff boats became regarded as elegant veterans and most owners began to take a real pride in their craft. The term Old Gaffer is a little misleading because many of the craft are quite new.

However it was a term that people found easy to remember and so helped the gaff revival. Races and rallies are now held in many places, notably The Clyde, Dartmouth and in Brittany. Certainly our East Coast race grew and within a decade there were eighty or more gaffers taking part.

The first record of Essex smacks racing was in 1783, but by the Victorian era most villages were holding annual races. Some of these were begun again after World War II for the few remaining smacks sailed for pleasure. The local smack and Gaffer races stimulated interest for more people to want to take an active part in restoration so that by 1977 there were at least 39 Essex and Kent smacks in sailing order. There was no break in time between the days when smacks (and Thames sailing barges) worked and the revival movement started so that it was not just the actual craft that were saved but the whole local maritime tradition has been kept alive.

Yet time has not stood still. Every fishing village had become packed with yachts which produced more revenue for the space they occupied than the larger wooden traditional craft. At Brightlingsea the Colne Smack Preservation Society have overcome this problem by leasing some mud berths off the local authority. This little haven is reserved for local smacks only. It is actually part of Aldous' yard where many of them were built. This is a very agreeable situation with local craft kept and sailed in the area they belong. Even then their future is far from being absolutely secure. People will spend a sizeable part of their income and life restoring a smack from a motor fishing craft or even abandoned hulk in a creek, but when circumstances force them to sell a fully restored smack no one locally wants them. They are sold as conventional yachts.

Two Essex smacks, both with low counter sterns for day oyster dredging in sheltered creeks have made long voyages. The *Iris* was sailed by her French owner, without an engine across the Atlantic and back while the *Mayfly* sailed round the world. Some smacks have come home, such as the *Lizzie Annie* which was brought back to Maldon by lorry from Wales by enthusiasts.

The growth of the smack fleet focused attention on the other Thames Estuary fishing craft, the bawley. These were totally different from the sleek smacks, they had enormous beamy hulls which required a lot of ballast to keep them down in the water, but provided a stable platform for the boiler for cooking the shrimps. The bawleys had a very lofty sail plan and a loose footed main. Yachtsmen were very worried by the loose footed main and all bawleys converted to yachts like the *Good Intent, Band of Hope, Prima Donna, Gladys* and *Doy* were given booms and gaff mainsails. The first to go back to the proper loose footed sail was the 24 ft (7.20 m) *Vivida*. She was probably built in about 1860 and rebuilt in 1958 and is one of the early clinker-built bawleys

(Cont'd. p. 127)

FAR LEFT

The 112 ft (33.60 m) Nova Scotian Bluenose II *built at Lunenberg in 1963 is a replica of the famous fishing schooner* Bluenose *built on the same yard in 1921. Even with charter work, the* Bluenose II *has not been able to finance herself completely and has been subsidised by the Province of Nova Scotia (Author's Collection).*

LEFT

The Clearwater *is a replica of the Hudson River trading sloop and her 3000 sq ft (278.70 sq m) mainsail is set on a 65 ft (19.50 m) boom. She was built by Harvey Gamage, South Bristol, Maine in 1969 to help publicise the ecological problem on the Hudson River. She now manages to support herself as a training ship (Ivan Butler).*

The former Norwegian fishing vessel Trygvason *is now earning a living as a charter vessel mostly based at Hamburg (Author).*

When the 43 ft 6 in (13.10 m) fischkutter Aurora, *built on the German Baltic coast in 1934 was rigged out for sailing, the American style lazyjacks were fitted to catch the mainsail when it was lowered. However the American single handed gaff sailer Harry Pidgeon wouldn't have lazyjacks in the interest of simplicity because in a tropical squall, when sail had to be got down quickly, anything which could foul the sail aloft might result in the yacht's loss (Author).*

The 46 ft (13.80 m) Hirta *and the three masted topsail schooner 135 ft (40.50 m)* Sir Winston Churchill *in the 1973 Clyde Sail Training Race. The* Sir Winston Churchill *was purpose-built in 1966 as a sail trainer and does excellent work giving young people a taste of the sea (Gilchrist — Author's Collection).*

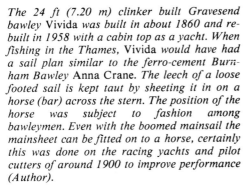

The 24 ft (7.20 m) clinker built Gravesend bawley Vivida *was built in about 1860 and rebuilt in 1958 with a cabin top as a yacht. When fishing in the Thames,* Vivida *would have had a sail plan similar to the ferro-cement Burnham Bawley* Anna Crane. *The leech of a loose footed sail is kept taut by sheeting it in on a horse (bar) across the stern. The position of the horse was subject to fashion among bawleymen. Even with the boomed mainsail the mainsheet can be fitted on to a horse, certainly this was done on the racing yachts and pilot cutters of around 1900 to improve performance (Author).*

which fished from Gravesend. There was once a whole fleet of bawleys operating in the Thames mouth from Bawley Bay, Gravesend and the very last working under motor was the 34 ft (10.20 m) *Thistle* until 1970. She was carvel built by Gill at Rochester in 1888 and was one of the Strood bawleys. Only these bawleys had mast cases for lowering their masts when they went above Rochester bridge. The *Thistle* later spent several years sunk to the deck in fresh water in the Thames but has since been refloated for restoration.

The round bottom bawleys were usually built in the same yards as the flat bottomed Thames sailing barges so that it is hardly surprising that the two types although very different in many ways, had many similarities. Some of the best bawleys were built by Canns at Harwich and they also built extremely well constructed barges. The Cann built bawley *Doris* is back under sail, while another Cann built bawley, the *Helen & Violet* is under restoration at Brightlingsea. Along with this is the Aldous built *Bona* and the *Saxona* which was actually built as a power craft. The *Lilian* is being restored at Maldon.

In North America the traditional sail revival cult has been largely centred on keeping the gaff schooner alive. When some of the smaller fishing and freight schooners could no longer eke out a living they were sold off as dude schooners for carrying passengers in the summer. Most of these are based in Maine and make weekly cruises around the islands in Penobscot Bay. Because of the wording of the law in the United States none of the dude schooners can have engines and instead they have powered yawls to push them into harbor. To help encourage interest in the classic North American schooner a Windjammer Day was started in 1963 for all the New England schooners to meet. New York has also started an annual Schooner Race with at one point the schooner yachts sailing virtually under the shadow of the high rise buildings of Manhattan.

The most famous schooner race of all was the International Fisherman's Trophy of the 1920-30s. The fierce competition between Boston and Gloucester, Massachusetts and the southern shore of Nova Scotia pushed the huge fishing schooners to their final point of development. The Trophy was modelled on the America's Cup so that after preliminary races one New England schooner one Nova Scotian schooner met to race for the Trophy. The ultimate winner of the series was the Nova Scotian *Bluenose* of Lunenburg which made her legendary throughout Canada. In 1970 schoonermen revived the race. By then, however, most of the huge fishing schooners had gone. Instead it was sailed between gaff schooner yachts. Comparisons between the old and the new champions show how the event has been scaled down. The 112 ft (33.60 m) *Bluenose* had an 81 ft (24.30 m) mainmast and a 53 ft (15.90 m) maintopmast and set 10,901 sq ft (1,012 sq m) of sail. A new Canadian champion, the 46 ft (13.80 m) *Kathi Anne II* built and sailed by David Stevens of Tancock Island, Nova Scotia has a 52 ft (15.60 m) mainmast and sets 1,040 sq ft (96 sq m) of sail. However the spirit of the event is kept alive.

OPPOSITE TOP:
Here in 1971 are two John Leather designed 19 ft (5.70 m) New Blossom Class yachts racing in the River Colne with the oyster smack Mary, *built in about 1900. The New Blossom Class was based on the West Mersea winkle brig, the Essexman's name for an open working boat. The prototype was* Island Blossom, *built in 1961 (East Anglian Daily Times).*

OPPOSITE RIGHT:
The topsail on the bawley Anna Crane *is not set properly, it should be closer to the mast and flat. The only difference aloft from the boom rig is the brail across the loose-footed bawley's mainsail (Author).*

The Essex oyster smack Martha Two *built by Aldous at Brightlingsea in 1876 seen sailing after restoration in her hundredth year. The working smack had a narrower forsail on a horse so that they didn't have to bother with a sheet. Aldous often built hulls which could be sold on completion for yachts or for fishing.*

The Essex stowboat smack Charlotte Ellen *was built in 1906 at Brightlingsea by Kidby. Charlotte Ellen was rerigged in 1977 to take part in the smack races and carries a sail area far larger than winter sprat fishing would have required. Before 1914 it was considered bad seamanship to ever sail with topmast up and no topsail set. Although lowering the topmast every time the sail came down was largely a matter of custom, it did make practical sense to keep down weight and windage aloft. Like the Victorian yachts the Charlotte Ellen has 'channels' projecting from the sides to give a wider spread to the shrouds. The bawleys didn't have channels which made working the stow nets much easier because there was nothing to catch on (Author).*

Often when traditional craft are converted to yachts they are spoilt in appearance and performance as sailing craft. One of the exceptions is the 48 ft (14.40 m) Duenna *which was actually built by Aldous in 1903 as the smack S.W.H. She became a ketch yacht in 1960 and then Laurie Johns rebuilt her as a brigantine. In 1970 she was bought by Egon Heinemann of Hamburg and she is seen here as a topsail schooner on the River Elbe (Author).*

The Gracie *CK46,* William & Emily (Odd Times) *CK 212 and* Iris *CK 67 at the start of the West Mersea smack race in 1969 (East Anglian Daily Times).*

The 1976 Colne Smack Race (L to R) ADC, Betty, Hyacinth, Lizzie Annie, Mary, Priscilla *and* Peace. *This race was revived in 1971 and the record time by 1977 for the 19.4 mile (30.60 km) course, the shape of which always gives one windward leg, is 3 hours 3 minutes sailed by* ADC *(Author).*

The Essex smacks 33 ft (9.90 m) Hyacinth *and 44 ft (13.20 m)* Shamrock *racing off Bradwell in 1971 (Author).*

At the same time as interest in actually sailing traditional craft to forge a link with the past was growing on the American North Eastern seaboard and in Western Europe, an old event was also revived on the West Coast of America. This was the San Francisco Master Mariners Regatta started again in 1965. The first of these races was held in 1867 as a Fourth of July attraction. This race was for the coastal schooners and work boats of The Bay and proved to be so popular that it was held annually until 1877. Subsequent races were staged in 1879, 1884, 1885 and the last one in 1891. The West Coast is very open and does not lend itself to engineless dude schooners. The craft which take part usually have a traditional sail plan, but as in the old days each one is sponsored by a shipping company as their representative.

CHAPTER TEN

New Generation Gaff

The gaff revival has led to two very distinct lines of thought. One section have bought and restored elderly gaff craft while another group have concentrated on producing new types of gaff yachts which incorporate modern materials and trends in design. For the vast majority of people who go afloat for a leisure activity, the gaff sail went out of favour in the early 1950s. There was never a complete break for throughout the following two decades there were a few new gaff yachts built and even some classes started, but they were supported by only a very small faction of the boating community.

New gaff classes started in Britain in the mid-1970s received much more support, although it is fair to say that this still only had a small corner of the boat market. In the Old Gaffers Races two craft which gave consistently good performances were the 21 ft (6.30 m) *Quiver*, before she was lost on a Brittany reef in 1971 and the 22 ft (6.60 m) *Fanny*, both of which were built as the Solent smacks which yachtsmen called Itchen Ferry types. In 1973 the *Tamarisk* class was started with a reinforced plastic hull based on the Itchen Ferry type. All had a gaff cutter sail plan and two 22 ft (6.60 m) hulls were built and about ten 24 ft (7.20 m) hulls. Apart from being a little heavy on their helm their owners found them satisfactory but they were more expensive than a bermudian yacht of the same size.

The 24 ft (7.20 m) Cornish Crabber was the first gaff class to enjoy a wide success. The Crabber came about because Peter Keeling and Roger Dongray were getting a lot of fun from sailing their Drascombe Luggers on the River Camel on the North Cornish coast, but they thought they would like to take it a little further and have a traditional boat 'with a lid on'. Roger Dongray, an architect by profession, had done a lot of research into local work boats and he blended this together to produce a Crabber, a gaff cutter with accommodation. It was intended as a boat for their own use and had to be shoal draught because the Camel dries out, but also this small river opens right out on to the fury of the North Atlantic so it was equally important that the Crabber could survive in rugged conditions.

The first Crabber, the *Sarah Jane*, was built of marine ply and was launched in April 1974. It seemed right away that they had struck a successful design so Westerley Boats, of which firm Peter Keeling is Managing Director, started to build another Crabber. Now two boats of the same hull design could be used to try out new ideas in sail plans by racing against each other. The major improvement was the fitting of a mainsheet track for better control of the mainsail shape. The second Crabber was shown at Southampton Boat Show in the autumn of 1974 and orders started to come in, particularly from The Netherlands. Only four marine ply Crabbers were built; on the fourth, the shape was taken off to start producing a GRP hull. In switching to GRP

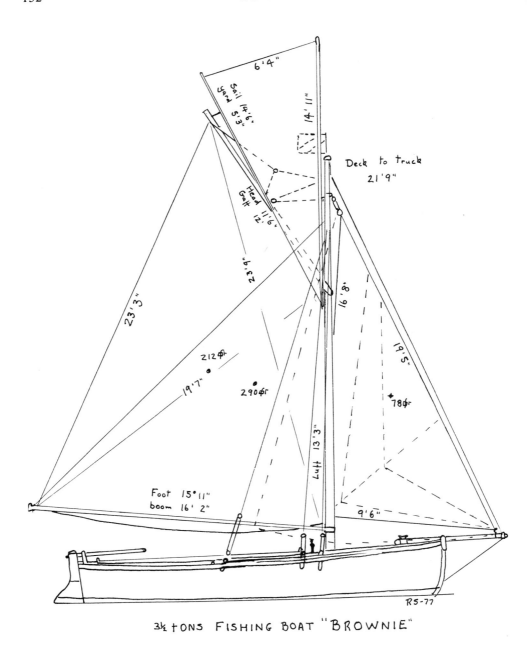

6'4"

Sail 14'6"
Yard 5'3"

14'11"

Deck to truck
21'9"

Head 11'6"
Gaff 12'6"

23'9"

23'3"

16'8"

19'5"

212 ft

19'7"

290 ft

78 ft

Luff 13'3"

Foot 15'11"
boom 16' 2"

9'6"

R S-77

3½ TONS FISHING BOAT "BROWNIE"

Sail plan of fishing boat Brownie *designed by R. N. Stone, 1925.*

about £1,000 was saved in producing each hull. Westerly Boats considered ferro-cement hulls only suitable for large 'one off' craft and not for a production line.

Within three years of the first Crabber sailing 120 new hulls had left Westerly Boats yard at Rock, Cornwall, not just for British owners but all over Western Europe. The Crabber's winning qualities are that she has all the characteristics of a traditional craft but has the sailing qualities of a modern family cruiser. The lightweight hull with a centreboard was influenced by a modern sailing dinghy, but the above waterline appearance is that of a working boat. But this has a purely practical function because the short counter stern gives a great deal of space which makes a really roomy cockpit. The low gaff sail plan makes her easier to control in strong winds than with a taller mast needed for a masthead sloop. The mainsail is loosefooted and has reef pennants and bee blocks, but all the fittings and material are contemporary yacht fittings. This means that the mainsail is lighter, but having the loosefooted sail does mean more work in reefing. The designer stresses that this is just what they originally wanted. They were bored by the mast head sloop and wanted 'more strings to pull'.

The same line of thought led to yacht designer Alan Hill of Burnham on Crouch starting the 32 ft (9.60 m) Burnham Bawley class. A client gave him an oil painting of two fishing bawleys and this inspired him to produce a ferro-cement hull class based on them. There was little attempt to over improve on the traditional hull shape, although the Burnham Bawley has a long keel of the later fishing bawleys. The great beam of the bawley hull with its Cann-style transom stern gives a fantastic amount of cabin space.

Anyone wanting plenty of cabin space in a very seaworthy hull shape usually looks to Colin Archer designed Norwegian sailing lifeboats. Thirty-five of these sailing lifeboats were built, mostly at Archer's Risor Yard. Most of them were later sold for yachts and one of them, the 48 ft (14.40 m) x 16 ft (4.80 m) x 9 ft (2.70 m) *Sandefjord* (No 28) was pitchpoled right over when running before an Atlantic gale in 1935. The ketch survived but a man and the mizzen were lost.

The 43 ft (12.90 m) ketch *Escape* was built on Colin Archer lines at Risor in 1936 and was the boyhood home of Paul Johnson. He had designed and built several yachts on which he had lived and made ocean voyages before returning to design a ketch inspired by the double ended *Escape*. This was the 42 ft (12.60 m) long 14 ft (4.20 m) beam *Venus*. Her fibreglass-foam-sandwich hull contains seven tons of fibreglass and eight tons of ballast. She is flush decked except for a raised cabin aft around the cockpit. The wide beam makes a comfortable home for her owner and his family. Also with the open deck she is a comfortable craft to sail but no waterslug when it comes to handling. Even with the heavy 18 oz (511 gm) canvas sail she averaged six knots in a 5,000 miles Atlantic crossing.

In the past it has been possible to buy a comfortable old sailing work boat and convert her into a 'dreamship'. Designer John Perryman of Lowestoft wanted to get back to the 'dreamship' idea when he started the Norske 35, 40 and 45 hull range (10.50 m, 12 m, 13.50 m) in length. He started with the Colin Archer redningskoite and pilot cutter in mind because this type was already famous for its seaworthiness, pleasant motion and weight carrying ability. The final Norske shape has above water appearance of a Colin Archer, but the under water lines of a 1960s ocean racer, so that combined in one hull is the performance of a modern yacht with the character of a traditional craft. The first Norske hull was constructed by Windboats Marine of Wroxham. This was an old established boat yard on the Norfolk Broads which went over to ferro-cement hulls in the early 1960s. At the time this was a very unfashionable switch since the boat building industry and the public were mesmerised by reinforced

The Cornish Crabber Vanitas *sailing on the Ijsselmeer shows the counter stern and roomy cockpit. The Crabber has the mainsail laced to the mast which was the traditional Dutch method while in Britain and North America hoops were used (Peter Keeling).*

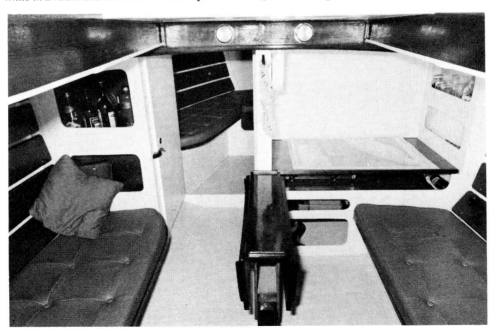

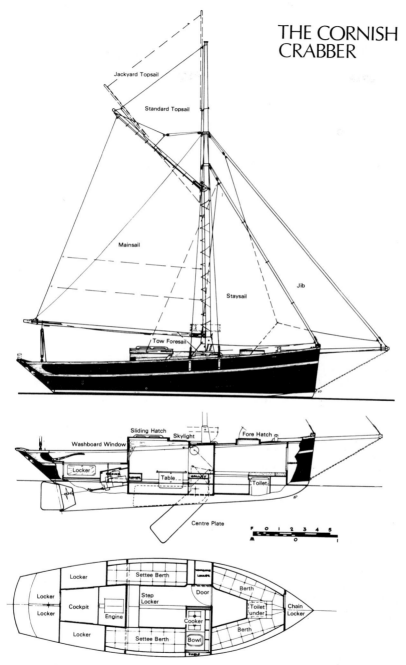

THE CORNISH CRABBER

Jackyard Topsail

Standard Topsail

Mainsail

Jib

Staysail

Tow Foresail

Sliding Hatch   Skylight   Fore Hatch

Washboard Window

Locker

Table

Toilet

Centre Plate

F 0 1 2 3 4 5
M   0   1

Locker   Settee Berth
                              Berth
Locker   Door
Locker   Cockpit   Step   Toilet   Chain
                   Locker   under   Locker
          Engine   Cooker
Locker   Settee Berth   Bowl   Berth

Plans of Cornish Crabber designed by Roger Dongray.

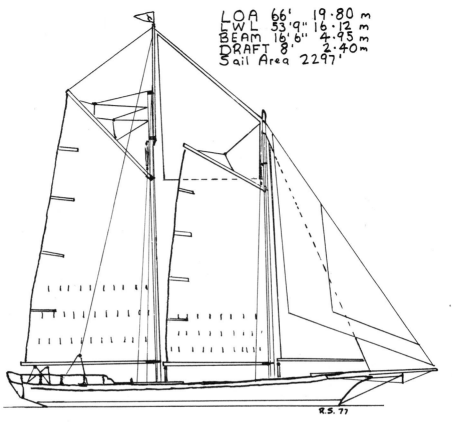

LOA 66' 19·80 m
LWL 53'9" 16·12 m
BEAM 16'6" 4·95 m
DRAFT 8' 2·40 m
Sail Area 2297'

R.S. 77

The tall sail plan of this 66 ft (19.80 m) schooner designed by Ferro-Marine Service, Burnham on Crouch, England is very much a new generation gaff sail plan.

plastic. In about 1964 New Zealand and American designers started to promote ferro-cement as being suitable for amateur building. Some of these amateur constructions had a very rough and ready finish and people wrongly assumed that ferro-cement hulls were all like that.

By the mid 1970s reinforced plastic was no longer the wonder product and the public was quite willing to accept ferro-cement. Meanwhile Windboats Marine had produced about 900 hulls, mostly for commercial work, but also specialised in large cruising yachts. The first Norske 35 completed had a gaff sail plan and I sailed on her shortly after her final completion in October 1977. On taking the tiller the first impression was that the Norske was very well balanced and would sail herself as long as the jib was set. When sailing close to the wind the sails shook, but the Norske was still happily crawling up to windward. Could it be that Norske's ocean racer lines made her sail closer to the wind than the gaff sail would allow? Designer John Perryman's comments on this were that the main and topsail had been cut too baggy on this cutter. The 8 oz (227 gm) terylene headsails needed to be cut to give a bent surface in order that they

The Memory Nova *is displaying her Old Gaffers Association number. These were started in 1975 because there were difficulties in identifying the small unregistered craft (The Boat).*

developed power, but the 10 oz (284 gm) main and topsail should have been cut to give a flat surface. Even then they would never be completely flat because the spars would bend, particularly the gaff and mast top. The Norske 35 with 5 ft (1.50 m) draft and 830 sq ft (77 sq m) of sail gave the impression of great power and the roomy ferro-cement hull cut out the water noise below.

In the original Perryman design the cabin top had round edges, an idea he got after seeing my Scandinavian cutter *L'Atalanta's* cabin top. This gives the cabin headroom, but takes the harshness off the usually square topped British and American cabin top. However Hanseatic Yachts, who completed the First Norske 35, had considered that the round edged cabin top would take too much time although they had finished the rest of the hull beautifully, complete with laid teak deck and other master pieces of the shipwrights art.

This was rather getting away from the 'dreamship' idea. However the seventh Norske 35 hull was constructed of wood, larch on oak with iron fastenings to a fishing boat finish in Southern Ireland and was to be known as the Rathlin Class. This was to have a pole mast with a jackyard topsail on a bamboo pole. Also many of the fittings were bought second hand, bringing the prices down and keeping the spirit of the original idea. Certainly wooden spars would give a great deal more character to the overall appearance. The first Norske 35 had tubular alloy spars with the mainsail going up on a trace on the mast and like the famous *Dyarchy* the jib headed topsail was also sent up in its trace. Having two topping lifts is the most practical arrangement for a gaff sail because it is very much easier to set a mainsail peaked up tightly if the weight of the boom is taken on the windward lifts. The Norske 35 has the topping lifts made up at the falls end to a cleat on the boom, in this way the topping lifts also form lazyjacks to help gather and control the sail on lowering.

The 19 ft (5.70 m) Memory class is the first day boat in the new generation gaff to find a wide market. The roots of this type of shoal draught sloop go back to the boats used by the police to patrol the River Colne oyster grounds. In the 1890s four centreboard sloops were built for the police by Aldous at Brightlingsea. These were different to the smacks and yachts, but in the 1920s Aldous built some similar small keeled cutters for oyster dredging and one of these the 27 ft (8.10 m) *Alando,* built in 1923 is still sailing after a complete restoration in 1974. Centreboard sloops were built at Brightlingsea for fishing, general hack boat work and racing, up to World War II.

It is probable that this local type would have been forgotten if Tony Robinson had not saved many of the old plans from being burnt at James Yard, Brightlingsea. He had never had anything to do with gaff boats, but was attracted by these drawings of the sloops with loose footed mainsails and jackyard topsails, so he decided to design himself a boat based on them. The most informative plans started with the 18 ft (5.40 m) centreboard sloop *Eileen* designed by R. N. Stone in 1922. She had carried a lot of weather helm so the next one, *Chiquita* had a slightly longer bowsprit and larger main. In 1925 the lines were increased to produce the 20 ft (6 m) fishing boat *Brownie* CK 30. To overcome the weather helm problem A. H. Robinson moved the mast further aft, reduced the mainsail in size and positioned a larger centreboard further aft. Next he built a wooden plug for a fibreglass mould in his back garden. Finally he made contact with Eric Bergquist who began producing the fibreglass Memory Class commercially and the first one was sailed in 1975.

In Denmark the renewed interest in building new wooden craft has come because the country has a plentiful supply of home grown timber and the construction of Denmark's large fishing fleet has kept wooden boat building skills very much alive. The

The Norske 35 is produced in ferro-cement to counterbalance the large gaff sail plan. A beamy GRP hull would have required a great deal more ballast which in turn would have created a jerky motion in a seaway. This Norske 35 has eyes in the mainsail for reef lacing to be passed through, a method of reefing used by the Lowestoft smacks and Broads yachts to avoid chafing but it was usually considered more laborious (Hanseatic Yachts).

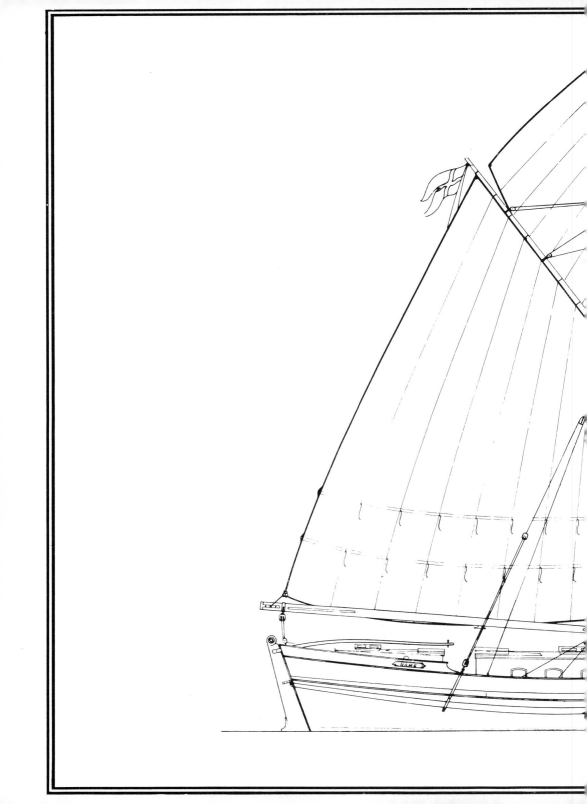

DEN DANSKE JAGT

Längde o.a.	*32'*
Bredde	*11'*
Dybgäende	*4'*
Sejlareal	*55 m²*

Skala 1:20

SKIBSBYGMESTER
MICHAEL KIERSGAARD
LODSVEJEN 32
09 225944
TROENSE

A wooden Danske jagt sailing near the Danish training ship Georg Stage *(Michael Kiersgaard).*

boat builder and designer Michael Kiersgaard has vigorously promoted the idea of yachts built on traditional craft lines and his 28 ft (8.40 m) to 39 ft (11.70 m) Danske Jagt type was started in 1974. A smaller jagt type had been produced previously by another Danish designer, but Kiersgaard's design was based on an original 1808 jagt which was a single masted craft which traded with apples, pears and vegetables between the islands and Copenhagen. The wide jagt transom stern makes the whole hull exceptionally spacious. Another feature which gives them room below is the square raised cabin top forward of the mast, a common feature in Danish and Swedish craft which makes the fo'c'sle very much more comfortable. Because of the conservation restrictions placed on Danish fishing fleets there has been a decline in orders for new boats so that yards at Marstal and Aerokobing have been glad to build new wooden Danske Jagts.

What then is the final conclusion that can be drawn on gaff sail? It would seem that the role played by gaff craft in the development of the democratic western society has been under rated in the past. However there does not, inspite of some predictions at the time of the fuel crisis, seem to be much possibility that gaff sail could return as true everyday working craft, but there is undoubtedly a place for them in specialised work such as for holiday charter work. There are to many worthwhile traditional gaff craft left for them all to be preserved as museum pieces. The best place for restored local craft is to keep them sailing, preferably in their home areas, as a way of keeping alive a feeling of local identity in the face of the featureless internationalism which now rolls across so much of our lives. Since a yacht's success should be measured by the amount of pleasure it brings to its owner and crew, gaff sail does have a real future in this field and there is still plenty of scope for it to go on progressing for leisure sailing.

Index